Stop Managing Stress!

20 Questions

to

Reclaim Your Life

Carol Woodliff & Karen Maleck-Whiteley

CONTENTS

Introduction 1

Question 1: Am I Taking Things Too Seriously? 11

Question 2: Am I Clinging to Control? 19

Question 3: Am I Making Assumptions? 27

Question 4: Am I Kind when I Talk To Myself? 33

Question 5: Do I Need To Have A Conversation? 41

Question 6: Am I Letting Others Push My Buttons? 49

Question 7: Do I Have Unrealistic Expectations? 57

Question 8: Am I Trying To Be Perfect? 63

Question 9: Can I Say No? 71

Question 10: What Am I Juggling? 83

Question 11: Am I The Queen of Multi-Tasking? 89

Question 12: Am I Last On My List? 97

Question 13: Am I Asking For What I Need? 101

Question 14: Am I Honoring My Feelings? 105

Question 15: Is This Event Activating Old Wounds? 113

Question 16: What Is The Next Small Step I Can Take Today? .. 119

Question 17: Where (Or Who) Is My Tribe? 125

Question 18: Am I Making Room for Joy and Play? 131

Question 19: Is It Time For A Big Change? 135

Question 20: Am I In Crisis? 143

Creating Your Personal Plan 151

If You Liked This Book: 155

About Carol And Karen..157

With Much Gratitude..159

INTRODUCTION

"Burying your head in the sand in the name of 'staying positive' is not a good strategy. Wearing blinders rather than looking right at what's going on right now is not the way to create your vision for tomorrow. Sculptors have to look at the block and begin cutting parts of it away before their vision emerges in the marble. Look directly at the block if you want to create the art."

Neale Donald Walsch

The term "stress management" is rather amusing. Who wants to spend time managing stress? Wouldn't you rather increase your ability to thrive in all sorts of circumstances? We would.

We are Carol Woodliff and Karen Maleck-Whiteley. After over twelve years of seeing private clients and teaching meditation, self-hypnosis and other techniques, we realized the traditional stress management strategies focused on the symptoms of stress. Deep breathing, getting a massage, taking a walk and many other techniques provide symptomatic relief. They are like temporarily taking the lid off the pressure cooker. They are great short-term solutions but these tools do not address the root causes of stress. They don't help us live powerful lives. Even more importantly, they teach us to believe stress is bad for us. Why is that a problem? Because what we believe about stress may determine how it affects us.

Researchers at the University of Wisconsin-Madison found that people who reported having high levels of stress and who *believed* stress would have a large impact on their health had a 43% increased risk of death. On the other hand, those who experienced a lot of stress but did not perceive its effects as negative were amongst the least likely to die as compared to all other participants in the study.[1] This study followed almost 29,000 people over eight years and asked participants to rate the level of stress they each had experienced over the last year as well as how much they believed this stress influenced their health—a little, a moderate amount or a lot. This study confirmed what we knew from working with clients:

---

[1]Keller A., Litzelman K., Wisk L.E., Maddox T., Cheng E.R., Creswell P.D., Witt W.P., "Does the perception that stress affects health matter? The association with health and mortality." *Health Psychol.* (Sept. 2012); 31(5):677-84.

> Your beliefs and expectations determine
> whether you see an event as stressful and they
> determine the effects of that event in the long
> and short term.

You can't erase all of the potential stressful events from your life. You wouldn't even want to. Deadlines can help you get things accomplished. A demanding boss can help you grow professionally. Moving to a new home, starting your dream business, writing your novel late at night after work or adding a baby to the family are joyful events that may also seem stressful. Tough traumatic events can have their share of lessons or growth opportunities when looked at in retrospect. You can't make all these events disappear from your life, but you can experience them in a way where you are not at their mercy.

Becoming aware of the beliefs and habits limiting your options and power is the first step in moving beyond stress management to living your life creatively and powerfully. You can see each event as giving you a blank canvas where you get to choose which colors and brushes you are going to use to create a picture that supports health and happiness. Your life becomes your art rather than a stressful burden to manage.

Two people can experience the same event. One person is able to handle it with grace and ease and another person can be so stressed they can't function. Some people are more resilient, others more sensitive, and some people have history that makes them more vulnerable to certain stressors. Fortunately, there are skills that can help you shift how you experience the world around you.

William James, the man considered the father of American psychology, said: "The greatest weapon against stress is our ability to choose one thought over another." This is the key to a better life and to the techniques in this book.

Are you creating stress by thinking that tends to make you a victim or a martyr? Are you ignoring events that require action? Are your thoughts helping you or hindering you? Be honest with yourself.

To claim your power to live your best life, you have to acknowledge what is happening in your life right now. You can embrace it, or confront it and change it; but ignoring what is happening will not help you.

Say you have been laid off from your job. That sucks! Or does it? Is it an opportunity? Are you scared? Are you worried about finances? Are you embarrassed? Angry? What are all the feelings and concerns you have? It is important to acknowledge all of them. You have a choice after you acknowledge the event and what feelings it brings up. You can get stuck in worry, or sit at home hoping someone will call you with a job. You can choose to believe you can rise above these circumstances and take action—revise your resume, reach out to your network etc. By questioning your assumptions and beliefs, you can see where you might be buying a ticket for the Stress Express rather than choosing to handle "what is" in a helpful and useful manner.

This is where the 20 Questions in this book come in. We've chosen these questions with some key premises in mind. They are:

- You have the power to change your life by questioning what you believe, see and experience.

- You can make positive choices helping you to become more powerful or negative choices giving your power away.

- Listening to your heart and connecting with the deeper essence inside you that you might call your soul or highest self will allow the best part of you to run the show.

- Self-care and love require setting boundaries and saying NO!

- This practice allows you to be more open to the good the Universe is sending your way.

We've been through our share of stressful events in life—financial challenges, illnesses and deaths in the family, being laid off from jobs, accidents, having businesses go through economic downturns—to name just a few. We use the questions in this book when we encounter challenging events, which test our resolve to stay centered. They work!

Are you ready to jump in?

Let's start with these important questions: Are you dealing with a stressful major life event that feels like a red alert crisis? Is your hair on fire? Does your life seem to be falling apart?

If the answer to any of those questions is yes, you may want to skip to QUESTION 20 for a guide on how to use this book when dealing with stress in crises.

Otherwise, let's begin with the first two exercise questions. Answer them quickly. Write down the first things that come to your mind. Don't worry. There is no right or wrong answers and no one is going to read over your shoulder or judge you by what you write down.

Many times, we hear from clients that doing this exercise brings up some guilt. You can love your elderly parent but be sad and stressed by how they are no longer the capable parent you once knew. You can love your child but this phase he or she is going through can drive you nuts. You know you shouldn't let these and other things bother you but they do. Being human is complicated and life is messy. Even if your answers feel ugly or embarrassing to you, be truthful about what stresses you out.

LIST 10 THINGS THAT ARE STRESSFUL FOR YOU:

1.

2.

3.

4.

5.

6.

7.

8.

9.

10.

Didn't have 10? Had more than 10? It doesn't matter you are simply creating a base line of the things you might like to work on in this book.

HOW DO YOU KNOW WHEN YOU ARE UNDER STRESS? What happens in your body? Your emotions? Your thoughts? Your relationships? List what you know now.

You already know a lot about what you call stress and how it affects you. Knowledge is power. Look directly at what you have been calling stress, and be open to the possibility it can be viewed differently. We will show you how to move beyond the idea of being controlled by stress and instead choose a life you can embrace.

Each of the 20 Questions addresses a theme that can add to perceptions, beliefs or feelings of stress. Simply reading through the list of the 20 Questions in the Table of Contents may have had some bells going off for you about patterns you may be intimately familiar with.

We invite you to go deeper and **"CHECK IN"** to explore what is going on in your life. Checking in is a call for reflection on where this theme might be operating in your life. It encourages you to find your "aha" moments and become aware of your current choices and behaviors.

We offer suggestions to help you **"TAKE ACTION."** Being aware of how your thinking limits your power won't give you your power back. You have to take action either with baby steps or big bold leaps. The size of the step isn't as important as the action step itself. Taking a step no matter how small shifts your focus and creates positive momentum.

Finally, each chapter ends with a **"REPEATABLE"** — a short phrase or mantra you can say to remind yourself you have the power to see your situation in a positive and useful way.

We encourage you to take the time to do the exercises. We admit we've read books that tell us to do exercises and we're tempted to skim past them. This is very similar to thinking about going to the gym instead of working out. We get results when we keep our promises to ourselves and do the work required.

Even small changes can dramatically shift your experience of stress, allow you to respond to life in a different way, and provide you with many more choices about your options and actions in any situation. Working with these questions on a regular basis increases your awareness of your options. These choices allow you to become the artist of your life—sculpting it in the way you choose rather than simply reacting to the things life throws at you. You can choose to reclaim your power. Stop focusing on managing the stress in your life and focus on choosing the thoughts and actions that help you align with who your spirit came here to be.

QUESTION 1:
AM I TAKING THINGS TOO SERIOUSLY?

"Do not take life too seriously. You will never get out of it alive." Elbert Hubbard

"Am I doing this right? Yikes, I just blew it! I better prepare for all the possible ways this could go wrong. Argh! This Life thing is hard!"

STOP!

Being human has many challenges but it is also hysterically funny. We may try to act as though we have "it" all together and we are so very cool and then that thing happens where we just can't be cool. We burp or fart at inopportune times. Our skirts get caught over our heads. We fall off our shoes in front of a live audience. We forget our boss' name when it is time to introduce her to our most important contact. The list goes on and on.

Humor often comes from pain and embarrassment. In those moments, you realize you have a choice of whether you are going to crawl under a rock or you are going to laugh. We always vote for laughter. Even if the laughter is simply, "Here I go again doing THAT thing and making myself crazy!"

Laughter is good for you. It is one of the great gifts we were given. There is nothing more joyful than a baby laughing. There is nothing more healing than a true, deep laugh. You may be familiar with the story of Norman Cousins who was diagnosed with an illness, which the doctor said would probably kill him and for which there was no treatment. With his doctors' consent, he checked himself out of the hospital and into a nearby hotel and began a laughing cure viewing a continuous stream of humorous films and other materials that helped him to laugh. He later said he could get two hours of pain-free sleep from 10 minutes of deep belly laughter--something painkillers were unable to do for him. If stress had somehow contributed to his illness, he believed positive emotions would help him feel better. He proved this hypothesis and recovered from his illness. His book, *Anatomy of an Illness*, is a classic, which advocates combating life-threatening illness through humor and patient participation in care.

Whether you are ill, facing a major loss or just going through life's daily challenges, finding the humor in those moments can be one of your greatest tools.

Throughout this book, we tell tales on ourselves. We share our "life is embarrassing" and "I can't believe I am doing this" moments--those moments when we forgot for a moment we had choices to see things in a different way. You can laugh with us; you can laugh at us, but please laugh! We all strive for the illusive "it" as in having "it" all together. When we accept we probably will never have all our stuff together and let ourselves laugh, we find the energy to begin again another day.

Sometimes we forget our funny bone. People who study acting, improvisation and standup comedy train themselves to look for the funny in all situations. One of Carol's friends who did standup for many years said, "It is all material."

Even in some very tragic circumstances, like the funeral of a loved one, there is often laughter as we remember the good times with the deceased person. This is as it should be. Laughter is medicine for the soul.

Carol: I recently had to help my beloved dog, Sadie, transition to the other side. She was old, tired and hurting. I knew it was the right thing to do. She passed peacefully in my arms and yet there was a big hole in my heart. The house was empty. I decided to wash her gently used toys to take to the animal shelter for other dogs to enjoy. One of the toys was a stuffed frog with a voice box that sounded like a frog ribbitting. When it came out of the washing machine, it sounded like a sick goat. I laughed so hard. Even though I was still grieving, the loss of my companion, a wave of, "It will be okay," washed over me.

Karen: Many years ago when I lived in Petaluma, I stopped at the bank to make an ATM deposit while on the way home from a long and trying day. When I started my car afterwards, it was running very roughly and making noises that made me worry if I drove it further, it might damage something. My husband was working in San Francisco and I did not want to wait an hour or more for him to come get me, so I got my handbag and workbag, went next-door to the drug store, bought a bottle of wine, and began my walk home. I didn't live too far as the crow flies—maybe a mile or so. However, if I wanted to walk on sidewalks, I would have to go twice as far to get out of the shopping center, cross the 101 freeway on a road overpass, go past my house to get to the entrance to the housing development I lived in, and then double back inside the development to get to my house. My home was on the very last street in the tract, back against the freeway.

I was wearing work clothes, pantyhose, and heels. With each step, my feet got sorer, and I got angrier about my day and my car, and more impatient to get home. I wanted this stupid day over. As I got to the other side of the freeway, it dawned on me I could see the chain link fence that curved around my yard. It was just across the freeway off-ramp I was now parallel to. It would be so much shorter to cut across the off-ramp, climb down and across the leafy drainage area between the off-ramp and my fence, and somehow scale the 6-foot chain-link fence. In a matter of minutes, I would be dropping down into my own yard, and thereby save at least 20 more minutes of walking in those darned heels.

So I went for it. Running across the off-ramp was a piece of cake. Negotiating the drainage ditch wasn't too bad. Then I got to the fence. I zipped my purse shut and threw it over. I got the toes of my pumps into the fence and was able to flip the workbag with the wine in it over too, and it dropped down into a flowerbed where it luckily landed upright. Now I just had to get myself over. With some effort (those shoes were never going to be the same!), I climbed and got high enough to get my leg over, and then neatly avoided the spiky top of the fence getting the second leg over so I could get my foot into the fence on the other side. This wasn't so hard! My toes really hurt by now, so I got brave and jumped down to the grass. I landed with my skirt hiked all the way up under my arms because the hem had gotten hooked on the top of the fence. Really?

As I continued to jump up and down trying to get it free, a car swung around the corner of my street, and headed straight down the block with its headlights pointed directly at me. I was spotlighted there, stuck on my own fence, skirt in the air, slip showing. I was mortified, but also burst out laughing. Somehow, I got my skirt down and was still smiling as I made it inside for that glass of wine. I felt silly, but was grateful not to be walking another mile. I have shared this story many times as a "make your friend feel better about what they did" tale. It never fails to help us laugh!

Carol: When friends share their stories, you often find you have lots of this "being human stuff" in common. When Karen told me her skirt story, I immediately thought of one of my own. Several years ago, I was asked to speak about hypnosis at a local medical school. It was a great opportunity for me and it was stressful. I wanted to do a polished, professional presentation differentiating hypnosis for life improvement from the hype and misinformation in movies and television. I prepared my presentation, made beautiful and informative handouts with a selection of the studies about the effectiveness of hypnosis as applied in medical settings. I arrived early dressed in skirted suit and heels. The classroom was set up amphitheater style with the audience sitting in rows ascending up with aisles going up the middle and both sides.

The professor, a doctor of osteopathic medicine, told me they were expecting a large turnout for my presentation and many of the students were interested in using hypnosis for helping them with their testing skills. The appointed hour arrived and the auditorium filled with the medical students. I began talking about the difference between stage and movie hypnosis and therapeutic applications as used in medicine and lifestyle support. The student doctors were taking notes and nodding. I had them in the palm of my hand. I walked up the stairs into the audience to take some questions and back down to the front of the room to present again. I ventured up the stairs a second time and I missed a step, and stepped back down onto the lower step wobbling off one heel, catching myself, turning the other ankle and tumbling down the stairs!

Mortified, I quickly stood up, smoothing down the skirt that was bunched up mid-thigh, and hoping I hadn't flashed anyone my underwear. "I'm okay! I'm fine!" I said to the few people who had come to my aid. I laughed, my face turning bright red with embarrassment and said, "You all are going to remember me now, aren't you?" I took a few deep breaths and finished the presentation.

Afterwards one of the professors, asked me, "Are you sure you are okay? Do you need us to look at your ankles?" I assured him I was fine. We stood talking for a few minutes then I packed up to head out to my car. As I was walking to my car, the adrenaline that had carried me through the presentation dropped out and I could feel the pain of two badly sprained ankles as I tried to limp to my car. "You are fine," I kept repeating and laughing to myself. Each step sent a message of pain up my legs as I shuffled to the car.

By the next morning, I could only crawl around my house because it was too painful to walk. It was something out of an "I Love Lucy" episode--trying to figure out how to lift myself from crawling to the toilet without putting any weight on my feet.

Even with falling off my own shoes and taking that tumble, I ended up with several clients from the presentation. They did remember me. One of those clients said, "You were so okay with falling down and laughing at yourself, I thought, this woman can help me with my test anxiety."

Little secret here—I'm a bit of a klutz. I walk into walls and that wasn't the first time I've fallen off my shoes. What's a gal to do? I could be mortified or I can laugh. I choose laughter.

CHECK IN

When you find the humor in a challenging situation, it often transforms the situation on the spot.

Some questions for you:

- Are you someone who has the natural talent of finding the funny in life's challenges? Or are you more serious?

- Do you tend to lose your funny bone when the going gets tough? Or have you just forgotten your innate sense of humor?

- Can you allow the possibility that what you are experiencing right now is "good material"? Can you imagine yourself telling a funny story about it down the road?

- Go back to the list you created of the things that stress you out. Is there anything on that list you can laugh about?

TAKE ACTION:

Laugh! It's good for you!

- See a funny movie or old favorite television episode

- Try Laughter Yoga or go to a comedy club

- Tell your story to a friend over a glass of wine or a coffee. Make sure you tell it emphasizing all there is to laugh about. Allow yourself to reconnect with your funny bone and lighten your load.

REPEATABLE

Laughter is good medicine!

QUESTION 2:
AM I CLINGING TO CONTROL?

"I cannot make the universe obey me. I cannot make other people conform to my own whims and fancies. I cannot make even my own body obey me." Thomas Merton

How much time do you spend trying to control the uncontrollable? The range of things you may be trying to control can be laughable if you can step back from the control center for enough time to consider what you are doing.

You can sit in traffic fuming because you planned to be somewhere in a half an hour and now it is going to take you an hour. You can try to cut around other drivers and honk. Still you will probably be no closer to your destination and you will be more frustrated because you are trying to force movement where it is not possible.

You can spend a lot of time trying to control your boss, your spouse, your children, or other people in your life and end up totally frustrated because they will not do things your way.

If you are the person who always has to take the lead and control the project, you may feel frustrated if others do not have the same view of the project or style of work as you do.

You may get upset when things don't happen in your desired timeframe. Do you hate your job but as many resumes as you send out, you haven't yet found a new one? Are you trying to sell your house and there don't appear to be any buyers who want your property? Are you dealing with a legal matter that just won't go away? The Universe has its own timing and you can make yourself miserable if you get stuck in the energy of "I want what I want NOW!" Sometimes no matter how much effort you extend, the message is "Wait, it isn't time yet!" Trying to control these instances will only add to your feeling of powerlessness. Work with what you can do in this moment; the rest is out of your control.

Being a "control freak" of any variety can increase your stress exponentially.

Carol: One week I had a friend from out of town stay with me while she was attending a conference. She repaid my hospitality by cleaning and doing laundry. I found myself standing at the linen closet refolding the towels she had laundered and muttering to myself about how the towels weren't folded the "right way" even though they fit in the linen closet quite nicely the way she folded them. I had a flashback to when my mother used to mutter how we kids hadn't done things the right way as she straighten the silverware lining up all the tines of the forks in the drawer. I didn't like seeing that in myself and when I took a step back, I had to laugh. People pay for housekeeping help and I had someone helping with the laundry for free. If I could let go of the need to control how it was done, I had one less task to do. I was spending precious time refolding towels that didn't need to be refolded and it was only my thought that there was a "right way" causing me stress. There are times when we are trying to control things that in the big picture aren't important. I know some of you may be thinking, "But there is a right way to fold the towels." It's your choice. I have better things to do in life than worry about the perfectly folded towel! This was one of things I was trying to control I could let go of and be happier.

Karen: A while back, my 20-year-old son got a speeding ticket. He was assigned a court date that didn't work well for him due to his class schedule. When he called the courthouse to change the date, he was told he could change the date one time, but he had to go to the courthouse and see the clerk at least 10 working days before the assigned date. In my usual "efficient" manner, I entered a reminder in my calendar and nagged him about it. Our conversations went something like this:

> Me: "Did you go to see the clerk to change your court date yet?"

> Son: "I'll take care of it!"

> Me: "You don't have much time!"

> Son: "I said I'll handle it! Geez Mom!"

After several of these conversations, I finally decided to let him handle it. He drove all the way to the courthouse to change the date, and was told he had missed the deadline and he would have to appear on the original date.

The mom in me still wants to protect and handle things for my sons even though they are both adults. Trying to control and micromanage them is not healthy for either of us. In the end, it is better to let them make decisions and take the consequences for what they do—good or bad. How is he going to become responsible for his own calendar if he doesn't experience the consequences of not following through? It is hard for me to let go but I know it is important. I'm sure many of you moms reading this can relate. When I try to control my sons' lives, I add more stress for all of us.

The serenity prayer often used in 12 step programs is a good tool for controlling types. "God grant me the serenity to accept the things I cannot change; courage to change the things I can; and wisdom to know the difference."[2] "Wisdom to know the difference" is the key.

The first step in dealing with control issues is becoming aware of what is within your control. The things you can control have to do with you—how you take care of yourself, the actions you take, the stories you tell yourself, how you choose to speak to yourself and others, and when you choose to let go.

If your habit is to focus on trying to change things that are out of your control like other people or events that have already happened, surrender! Give up trying to control the uncontrollable. Let go and work with *what is* rather than forcing

---

[2]Serenity Prayer by Reinhold Niebuhr.

it to be something else it isn't or can't be. Here are some ways you can phrase that surrender:

- "I can't figure out how to change this. I'm going to let this go and focus on what I can control and put my best efforts there."

- "I can't control this event or person, so I'm asking for God, the Angels, or the Universe to handle this one and trusting all will be well!" (Choose the reference to the Higher Power or Spirit that works for you.).

- "Help me let go of what I can't control!"

CHECK IN

Go back to the list you created at the beginning of the book of the things that stress you out. Identify where you have been trying to control things not within your control or the silly things that don't need to be controlled. Notice how much of your life force is spent trying to control the uncontrollable.

Questions for deeper exploration

- Where are the situations or projects I am most likely to be a control freak?

- Am I uncomfortable delegating or asking for help?

- What am I taking on because I believe no one can do it like I can?

- Where am I focusing on controlling things that don't matter?

- Where am I trying to control things that are not my business to control?

- Am I fighting the timing of the Universe and upset because things aren't happening as quickly as I want them to happen?

Notice how those thoughts can add up to more stress.

TAKE ACTION

Pick one area where you know your control freak is acting up. What needs to happen? Do you need to let others handle their own business? Do you need to stop nagging? Do you need to find ways to handle lines and traffic? What is one control area you can practice with this week? Once you have chosen your target area, write it down. Come up with an alternative plan. Here are some examples:

- Instead of fussing about the traffic and my commute, I am going to download some books to my phone so I can play books on tape as I commute. I surrender to the traffic.

- Instead of trying to control my adult children, I am going say my opinion once and then let them do what they need to do. I surrender to their need to walk their own path.

- I am going to choose to notice where I make extra work for myself by stepping in to take control and I'm going to repeat to myself, "Not everything needs to be done by me." I surrender to the fact not everyone works the way I do.

REPEATABLE

Releasing what I do
not need to control
creates peace,
freedom and power.

QUESTION 3:
AM I MAKING ASSUMPTIONS?

"Your assumptions are your windows on the
world. Scrub them off every once in a while,
or the light won't come in." Isaac Asimov

Do you sometimes operate under the misconception of an
assumption rather than verifying the facts? Truth is we all do at
times. It is part of our human tendency to fill in the gaps in our
knowledge. Often times, those assumptions lead us to act out of
false information. We make assumptions about other people
and why they are doing what they are doing. We assume the
way we've always done things is the best way. We assume we
have the best approach or idea, and find out if we had only
gotten more input or involved others, things might have been
easier. We assume all our deadlines are real, even when we were
the ones to choose the timeframe and made up the deadline in
the first place. We know we are right. You get the idea. We
often forget we are making assumptions and move forward
without questioning ourselves.

Carol: I often do more work than I have to because I dive in and assume I am the one who has to take care of things and make sure that everything is done. When I was working as a paralegal case manager in a law firm, a project had been on my "to do" list for a week. By the time, I started working on it at 3 p.m. the day before the project was due, I knew at least 12 hours of work were required to complete the project by its 9 a.m. deadline. I got to work assuming all the members on my team were equally busy. I finished the project at 4 in the morning and went home to grab 2-3 hours of sleep before turning around and going back to work. The next day I came into work to an email from one of the attorneys apologizing for not letting me know they had settled the case. It seems everyone else knew this at 4 p.m. the afternoon when I assumed I had to work all night. I uttered some bad words as I clutched my coffee trying to wake up after only getting 3 hours of sleep. Knowing how priorities often change, I could have verified the 9 a.m. deadline was still firm before I started the work. If I had called to check in with any of my teammates to see if they could help, I might have heard the case had settled. Assuming I had to do the work and there was no one to help me, resulted in me pulling an all-nighter when I didn't have to do so.

It was a lesson I often repeated to those I mentored. Always check in before you expend lots of effort if time has elapsed between getting the assignment and when you start it. Don't assume other people have communicated with you that the project needs have changed.

WHAT
DO YOU
SEE?

When you assume you know what someone is thinking or why someone is behaving in a certain way, there is a good chance you are creating a story much bigger than what is happening. Are you turning the innocent bug on the floor into a bigger monster than it is? So many things we believe to be true are often based more in our imaginations than in fact.

Our assumptions are like spells we cast on ourselves. We start creating a world where people are doing things intentionally to hurt us or where we have to do things ourselves, where we are unlovable or whatever other story you might spin. The spell can be broken by asking yourself, "Is what I believe true? Do I know it is true? How do I know? How do I act when I believe this? Could I believe something else?"[3]

Karen: I had a friend "Betty" who worked for a high level executive. In meetings, the executive began to be less communicative and would often frown as people contributed their ideas. Betty and many of her co-workers decided the executive must be very unhappy with their performance or their ideas. They worked harder and harder to make him happy, but

---

[3] We give credit to The Work by Bryon Katie for these questions.

he still seemed angry all the time. The staff was increasingly on edge; trying to please this man and feeling as though they were not delivering what this manager wanted. They started to wonder if there was something going on with the company that he wasn't telling them. The truth came out several weeks later when the executive showed up wearing hearing aids. Far from being angry or upset with his staff, the executive had been trying very hard to concentrate and hear—especially with higher pitched women's voices. The concentration was what put the scowl on his face. His mainly female staff had incorrectly assumed his expression had something to do with them or something they were doing, instead of his own internal struggle. Think of all the stress created by the stories those women had been telling themselves—stories not based in fact but in incorrect supposition. There is a reason for the old saying, "Assume creates an ASS out of U and ME." How often do we assume we know what people are thinking by their facial expressions or body language?

Carol: Many years ago, my boss took me aside after a meeting to question me about why I didn't like the project plan that we had developed in the meeting. I was confused. I asked, "What made you think I didn't like the plan?" She said, "You were frowning and looking disgusted!" I was caught! I was disgusted at how long the meeting was going on and had spent the last part of the meeting trying to figure out what I needed to buy at the grocery store for dinner. Since it was going to be my responsibility to carry out the project, she wanted to make sure I was onboard. I had already created my plan for the project and had moved on in my mind to dinner while the rest of the group discussed the project for another 20 minutes. I told her I had been working out the details of the plan in my mind and left it at that. My boss had mentored a good skill. She saw something that she thought meant one thing and she verified her assumption before going back to her office with an untrue story about me not wanting to help with or not liking the project.

In his book *The Four Agreements*, Don Miguel Ruiz shares four agreements based on Toltec teachings that form a powerful code of conduct. One of those agreements is "Don't Make Assumptions." Every time we make assumptions, we are operating on potentially faulty information. By finding the courage to seek the truth, we can transform our lives. (If you haven't read *The Four Agreements*, we highly recommend it!) When you commit to examining where you are making assumptions or telling yourself stories, you might be surprised at how much of your stress stems from things that are not even true.

CHECK IN

Here are some questions you can ask yourself about the assumptions you may be making.

- Am I am imagining things that might happen?

- Am I projecting negative fantasies?

- Am I making up stories about other people's motives?

- Have I checked out my belief or am I making an assumption?

- Do I have the facts?

- Are my expectations/assumptions causing me trouble?

- Can I think of other just-as-likely scenarios?

TAKE ACTION

Find one area where you can verify whether the assumptions you are making are true. Be courageous. Ask the question that needs to be asked. Notice what changes for you as you practice verifying your assumptions.

REPEATABLE

Release assumptions
and find the truth.

QUESTION 4:
AM I KIND WHEN I TALK TO MYSELF?

"Be careful how you are talking to yourself because you are listening." Lisa M. Hayes

Do you talk to yourself in a way that helps you feel good and do better? Do you say hateful or hurtful things? How you talk to yourself affects your emotional and physical responses and the situation itself. Self-talk can be a source of stress, or it can be the source of empowerment.

Karen: I worked in the corporate end of big retail for over twenty years. In retrospect, I can now see I absorbed a mindset from the environment, which turned into my own self-talk about my job, myself, and even my outside life. Everything management wanted was *important*. Lots of situations were *urgent* or *critical*, action had to be taken *immediately*, and I was *essential* to what was going on at any given time. I would say these things to myself as I drove to work on my days off because I believed I was one of the essential people who needed to be there to solve the critical issues immediately. When I looked at how I was operating, it occurred to me if I got hit by a bus, the giant company I was a part of would go on, pretty much without missing a step. I was not essential.

I also recall noticing at one point our absurd use of language related to what we sold. One season, the color red was *important*. Another time, we had to send an entire *critical* imported shipment of skirts to be cut off and hemmed shorter because they were *essential* to the assortment and the new hem length was *important*. We paid a premium price for these alterations because it was *urgent* they hit the sales floor yesterday. We were spending more money than the skirts were worth to get this done, but since they were *essential*, I didn't feel I should say anything about what a bad business decision this seemed to be. None of us did, we just got the skirts done. Clearly part of my self-talk back then was, "These people must know more than I do," and saying that caused me to discount my own logical thinking. Seriously. Solving hunger and homelessness is important; not the color red, a particular hemline, or Italian ceramics for home decor. This sort of marketing speak may have told our customers about the season's trends, but as corporate and personal self-talk, it did not help us make better decisions and it often made me feel bad or stuck in an impossible situation.

Carol: Sometimes it is easier to see how this sort of self-talk causes problems when we witness it in others. When I heard a friend say, "My life is over" when her spouse decided to leave the marriage or another friend say, "This is the worst thing that could happen to me," when she lost her job, I understood they were expressing their pain, heartache and fears. However, as a life-long student of human behavior, I also noticed that other friends who had a different form of self-talk seemed to recover faster. Another friend going through a divorce who said, "I'm heartbroken and I don't know how to put myself back together," seemed to move on faster than the friend that said her life was over. I noticed in the second friend's language she was already looking for the solution, "how to put herself back together." Another friend who lost her job said, "I know it will probably turn out to be a good thing but right now I'm worried about finances and how this will all work," found a job faster than the "This is the worst thing to happen" friend.

Observing these kinds of language choices in others made me look at how I talked to myself. Often in how I talked to myself, there was a lot of blame and "shoulding" on myself. "I should be farther along than I am with this project." It doesn't help me get the project done; it only makes me feel bad about myself. Rephrasing the statement to, "I want to clear some time to focus on the project so I can have it done by September," is a lot more empowering than, "I should be farther along by now."

When something unexpected happens, do you say to yourself: "This is a disaster!" or do you say, "We'll have to re-evaluate what is needed now and adjust"? The key here is to be a good coach for yourself rather than a bully. Stating the facts in a kind, compassionate way helps you take the next steps. If you were going to choose a companion to be with you 24 hours, what do you want that person to say?

> This is the worst thing that could happen!
>
> You'll never get this done!
>
> You are a moron!
>
> This is impossible!

Or

> This is a problem we will have to deal with.
>
> This is taking longer than we had hoped. We need to think about how we can get it done faster.
>
> We made a mistake. How can we fix it or what have we learned for next time?
>
> This is a tricky situation. We need to figure out a solution.

Notice the energy shift in those statements. Look more deeply at those first four statements. It is easy to imagine catastrophes or to blow a problem up into a tragedy in your mind. But if you think about any problem, you can probably find there are worse things that could happen. It may be taking longer than you hoped to get a project done, but if it is important and needs to be completed, you will most likely finish it. It is highly unlikely you would be reading this book if you truly were mentally challenged. Focusing on the idea something isn't possible isn't going to help you find a solution to the problem.

When you talk to yourself, are you a helpful companion or a bully or naysayer? Are you exaggerating? Are you using "always" or "never" statements, which may not be correct? Are you saying, "I have no choice," or, "I have to," when you do have a choice, or when you simply don't like your choices? Does what you say help you to become a better person, do better next time or get your work done? Or are you beating yourself up? Would you talk to a child or a friend the way you talk to yourself? Probably not. We often talk to ourselves in ways we would never talk to others.

Example: If you hear yourself saying, "This is a disaster," check to see if you have a problem of the magnitude of a hurricane or major earthquake. You might say instead, "This is not what I planned on doing today, but I'm going to ask for help and make the best of it." This doesn't negate you have a problem but it puts you in a problem-solving mode.

Example: If you hear yourself saying, "I'm such an idiot!" or, "I'm a big fat slob!" think for a moment of whether you would consider it appropriate for someone else to say that to you or for you to say it to someone else. If you wouldn't find it appropriate to say to someone else, you should consider rephrasing what you are saying to yourself.

Think and speak in a calmer and kinder way and you'll feel calmer. When you feel calmer, your perspective is improved and you are better able to see ideas and factors you couldn't before. You can also better look ahead and more effectively plan, which is one of the keys to avoiding many crisis situations.

If you are in a crisis, how you talk to yourself can help you move through it. Saying things like, "Deal with the most important thing today and let the rest go," or, "You just have to get through the next 5 minutes," or, "This is temporary and will get better," or, "This is painful, and I'm doing the best I can right now and I'm not going to beat myself up for not being able to do the things I can do in better times," may help you keep moving through whatever the crisis is with less stress. When you are in a crisis, being kind to yourself and managing your personal expectations are the key. Question 20 shares more information about dealing with crisis situations.

At our core, human beings want to be seen, loved and respected. What human being is perfect? Not any we know! By definition, being human means making mistakes and learning as we go. What would shift if you treated yourself with the love and respect you give to friends and family? Most women we know are much better at giving this sort of love and respect to others than themselves.

Florence Scovel Shinn, an early metaphysical writer, reminded us that, "Your Word is Your Wand'—the very words we say are "filled with magic and power!" We often cast "negative spells" on ourselves. Apply a twist on the golden rule here—treat yourself the way you would have others treat you. Remember the power of the words you say to yourself—especially when you are wielding them as a weapon! You can just as easily use them to heal and strengthen yourself.

CHECK IN

Write down some examples of your self-talk. If you have trouble identifying what you say to yourself, take a day and listen to your internal dialog. Jot some notes and then answer the questions below.

- Could you speak to yourself in a more accurate and kind manner?

- Would you talk to a friend the way you are talking to yourself about this issue?

- Is there a more useful or helpful way to talk about the situation?

- What self-talk have you absorbed from your environment? Is it true for you today?

- What self-talk can you change now?

TAKE ACTION

Rephrase two of your common self-talk statements into more helpful statements and write them down.

Examples:

- If you catch yourself saying something like, "This will never get done!" try something like, "This is taking a lot longer than I thought it would. I might miss my deadline. I need to see if I can negotiate a new deadline or get some help."

- If you are saying something like, "I'm such an idiot!" substitute instead, "I made a mistake. How can I fix it?" or, "Well, at least I learned what not to do in the future." Or you can address these negative statements directly and tell yourself, "Not true! I am smart enough to deal with this."

Practice catching yourself when you say something mean or unhelpful and rephrase it on the spot.

REPEATABLE

Kind words make it safe to be me.

QUESTION 5:
DO I NEED TO HAVE A CONVERSATION?

"Having difficult conversations is one of your fundamental responsibilities in living. Difficult conversations are the very essence of love, intimacy, and generosity. And every time you postpone or avoid one out of fear you are wasting your precious life, failing in your responsibilities to others, and acting out of cowardice." From the blog Made of Metaphors[4]

Do you spend a lot of time dreading a difficult conversation with someone and putting it off as you go over all the possible scenarios again and again? Do you avoid the tough conversations entirely? Are you holding onto something that happened a long time ago and you never addressed? Do you have lots of, "I wish I had said something" moments?

---

[4]http://madeofmetaphors.com/difficult-conversations.

You may think by avoiding the conversation, you are reducing your stress. In actuality, you may be pushing the stress to the back burner and letting it simmer. You may think you are preparing for the conversation when you are worrying instead of getting it over.

Carol: I was 36 and dating a great guy. The only problem was my "let's get serious" clock was ticking and it seemed he was happy dating a couple of times a week. As much as I knew he cared for me, I felt something was missing. I knew I should have the talk but I kept putting it off, hoping by not putting pressure on him, he would come around. After all, people fall in love in their own timing. I started not sleeping well when we were together. I knew deep inside having the conversation would probably end the relationship, so I held off. We went on vacation together and we were visiting a winery and the person hosting the wine tasting for us, said, "This is a great mid-priced wine. It would be good for an event like a wedding." My guy replied, "Oh we aren't going there!" And I still didn't have the conversation. So many things about this guy were great. Except he wasn't in it for the long haul. Back home a few more sleepless nights and I finally admitted I needed to have the "where is this relationship going" conversation. I was hoping for a happily ever after but I got:

> "I'm not done dating. I think I need to date other people."

> "Date other people? Are you dating other women now?"

> "No but I can't imagine getting married again without more dating."

There it was. The fantasy I had created crumbled and the words came out of my mouth, "You are done dating me!"

Heartbreaking, but at least I was no longer in denial of how our timing was off. Even with the heartbreak, I slept better at night.

Karen: I had to give an employee a difficult review. I thought about all the possible ways the woman would react and got all my answers ready. I characterized this as good preparation.

I opened the review by saying: "I am sorry to have to tell you your review is not very good. There are several things we have to talk about."

I was completely surprised when she said, "Thank you for being honest with me. I know this isn't the right job for me, and I've been sitting in my cubicle thinking about how unhappy I am. I see now I need to get busy and make a change."

As we talked further, she made some plans to look for another job, and the session turned into a positive coaching discussion. In all of my mental rehearsals, I had not anticipated this outcome. I noticed I had only thought of all the negative things I might encounter. The experience taught me if I was going to anticipate various outcomes, I should also entertain the positive possible outcomes and not just prepare for the negative.

Having the difficult conversation at home, work and other relationships, puts us in integrity. How can we have good relationships with others when we are not having the important conversations?

The spiritual principle here is "speaking your truth." When your feelings and personal truths are not communicated honestly, they cause pain and stress. You feel the pain of suppression and others feel your lack of authenticity even if they aren't aware enough to label it as such. It is much healthier to find a way to speak up and say how you feel and release the pent up energy.

We are not talking about dumping on people. Speak your truth from a spirit of building trust and caring. The universe will support you when you come from the heart and compassionately share your truths and are willing to hear the truth of others.

We do want to issue a caution. Speaking your truth does not mean you need to say every thought in your head. You might also need to give yourself a time out to move out of emotional reactions and consider what you need to say. Sometimes when you reflect on an event and give yourself a little breathing room, you realize you don't need to say anything and you can let it go.

You know when you are avoiding a conversation you need to have. Those unspoken truths will absolutely continue to cause stress until you handle them.

There are many books written about having difficult conversations. We encourage you to explore those books or workshops if this is an area you'd like some support. Here are some tips you can apply right away.

- Take some time to get clear about what you want to happen in the conversation.

  o Do you want your feelings heard?

  o Do you want someone else to change their behavior?

  o Do you need to set a boundary?

  o Do you need to give bad news?

  o What does this conversation need to accomplish?

  o What would the best outcome look like?

  o What would be an acceptable outcome?

- A great tool to use is the "When you . . . I feel . . . Would you . . .?" construction. For example:

  o When you say you are okay with the decision we made in this meeting and then I hear from others that you aren't supporting it to the staff, I wonder what is going on. Would you be willing to tell me what changed between your agreement and your later conversations with the staff? Would you agree in the future to come back and talk to me if you have reservations after the meeting?

o   When you yell at me in front of my co-workers, I feel embarrassed and unable to process the feedback you are trying to give me. Would you be willing to agree to have those sorts of conversations in private and use a civil tone of voice?

o   When we come home from work and you spend the evening watching television, I feel ignored and unloved. Would you be willing to spend 15 minutes cuddling on the couch and talking with me about our days after we decompress a bit?

- Be willing to ask the tough question on your mind. For example:

o   Two months ago, I received a stellar review, but in the last month, it feels to me like something has shifted. My commitment to my job is the same but now it feels like I can't do anything right. Has something changed in the corporation I don't know about?

o   In the last few months, I have felt that you have been short with me. I feel sad our relationship doesn't feel as close. What is going on?

- If you need to have a conversation when you are upset or aren't completely clear about your feelings, tell the person upfront.

o   I need to talk with you about something that is bothering me and I'm not sure how to articulate it, so it may not come out as clearly as I would like. When you said, _____, I felt like I had been punched in the gut and got scared something was wrong. Can you explain what you meant?

- Ask for a break if you feel it is needed. It's okay to regroup or let others cool down.

  o I am getting emotional here because this conversation is important to me. I'd like a break to regroup before we continue.

  o It's obvious we are both upset. I think we should take a break and come back to this discussion later when we can talk calmly.

None of these communication tips guarantees you will make another person see your point of view or change. Remember other people are not within your control. In expressing yourself in a manner aligned with your truth, and being willing to listen to others do the say, you have done everything you can toward the goal of having an honest relationship.

CHECK IN

- What conversations are pending in your life?

- How much energy are you spending when you have the conversation in your head? Is there one you have been having over and over?

- What truths have you not communicated that would be better said?

- Is the thing you feel you need to say important to say, or are you feeling activated and feel the urge to dump those emotions? If the answer is, "I need to vent or dump," use caution as this may not be the time to communicate!

TAKE ACTION

Tackle one of your difficult conversations. BE BRAVE! Speak your truth with kindness and clarity.

If you need to vent or dump emotions, ask an uninvolved friend to be the "listener." Be clear you are venting, and establish a stopping point. "I need you to let me vent for 15 minutes!" Venting can be helpful but prolonged venting keeps you focused on the negative energy and make you a victim or martyr. Don't do it! Release the energy and then move toward finding solutions.

Remember to be a "listener" for your friend in return when he or she needs it.

REPEATABLE

Withholding my truth injures my relationships and me.

QUESTION 6:
AM I LETTING OTHERS PUSH MY BUTTONS?

"No person, no place, and no thing has any power over us, for 'we' are the only thinkers in our mind. When we create peace and harmony and balance in our minds, we will find it in our lives." Louise L. Hay

We often say other people cause us stress. Indeed, there may be people who are toxic and you might be better off staying away from them. But it is important to acknowledge even those toxic people, do not *force* you to you feel any particular emotion. It is your expectations of others and the assumptions you make about why they are doing what they are doing that causes you to feel a certain way. The good news is you can change your expectations and assumptions, and you can *choose* how you want to respond.

Think for a second about someone difficult who pushes your buttons. Now try this:

First say this to yourself: "How dare he/she treat me that way?"

Now say: "I wonder what happened in his/her life that makes him/her act that way?"

How does each statement make you feel? One statement makes you a victim. The other statement moves you to a position of empathy and power. When you look at it this way, it is obvious which question is most helpful. Which one puts you back in the driver's seat? We don't know anyone who hasn't let others push a button or two. It's human to have these reactions but we can reclaim our power when we choose how we label what the other person does.

Carol: In my law firm management career, I was often the one who got the phone call that an attorney was behaving badly and screaming at a staff member. It was my job to diffuse and solve whatever was going on. In the beginning I'd think, "Why do these people have to be such jerks?" I was walking into the situation confrontationally with my defenses up and adding more negative energy into an already charged situation. I was taking their behavior personally as though they were choosing to yell to mess up my day. When I asked a different question, "What could be happening that they would act this way?" I noticed the meltdowns happened when the attorneys had been working hard with very little sleep, not eating and were getting pressure from all sides—work and home. I was able to separate myself from the situation. I decided to think of these upset people like children who were over tired, hungry and over-stimulated. When I viewed the screaming person as overwhelmed rather than intentionally being mean, I could also respond in a way that helped everyone. I could fix their problem with something as simple as lending a kind and sympathetic ear or making sure they got some food while I also helped iron out any technical or staffing issues the attorney had. I created so much trust that I had their best interests in mind that the attorneys would automatically relax when I walked in the room and my life got much easier.

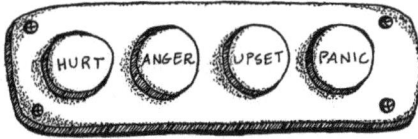

Karen: When I was a teenager, I walked into the living room at home to find my mother visiting with several visibly upset friends from our church. It turned out that a man we all knew had died unexpectedly, and the scheduled committee meeting had turned into a session of shared grief. I, too, was upset by the news. Inexplicably, my mother chose that very moment to show me a pattern she thought I would like her to sew for me.

"What do you think of this dress for school?"

It was not at all something I wanted to wear, and before I could stop myself, I blurted out: "I think it looks like s*&t!" and I stalked down the hall to my room.

As a normal adolescent, my mother pushed my buttons often but even I couldn't believe the word came out of my mouth in front of five church ladies. It was so unlike me. Our mother/daughter disagreements were aired in private not in front of company. Looking back, I realize I was shocked by the news of our friend's death, and I was in that teenage time when we are supposed to pull away from our parents. Just the same, I was horrified and embarrassed enough that it remains clear in memory today.

Consider the source of your reaction. If the person who gets you riled up reminds you of the way your sibling used to taunt you, or a hurtful ex-friend, you may find you are unfairly ascribing someone else's qualities to the person. This is a sign we have some healing and forgiveness work to do. This forgiveness is not for the person in front of us right now, but for our past. Until we do the work to heal those wounds, versions of your parents, that sibling, friend or ex-lover will continue to show up in your life. Even if you aren't ready to do the deep healing work, the awareness that the current person is a shadow of another negative experience can free you to deal with the current situation with more options.

Ultimately, you can choose not to be activated. You take back the power you have been giving over to someone who is intentionally trying to rile you when you choose to not let them have control over your responses. It takes practice. Remembering you are in charge of how you choose to feel and respond is one of the most empowering shifts you can make.

This isn't always easy. Living and working with other people is messy. People have different needs and are going to irritate each other from time to time. You are not going to eliminate all the negative people from your life and if you did you might be cutting out opportunities for your growth. Those people call us to tap into our most loving, patient, boundary-setting selves.

Sometimes we pre-push our own buttons thinking about what others will think, say or do. When you are afraid of conflict you often get upset thinking about a situation that hasn't happened yet. Sometimes you may feel like you are in a "damned if you do, damned if you don't" situation where you know you might be facing conflict no matter what you do. If you feel like you will meet disapproval or resistance no matter what you do, this frees you to pick an action or direction that you feel is most ethical, most right for you or best for all. Don't let your fear of the bullies or fear of letting others down push your buttons. Choose what is aligned and true for you and be brave enough to state your truth in spite of the potential feedback.

An old African proverb says, "When there is no enemy within, the enemies outside cannot hurt you." Being triggered by others is a calling to practice finding what needs love and kindness in the situation. When you feel less than loving or are triggered by someone else, there is an opportunity to see what needs healing, love and understanding within yourself. When people are acting in an unloving manner, they are sending out a cry for loving understanding, not judgment. Sometimes we do have to draw boundaries and take care of ourselves and we can only love someone when we get distance. Practicing love when you have your buttons pushed can feel like graduate school spiritual work. It isn't easy but it can shift everything for the better.

CHECK IN

Ask yourself the following questions:

- Is this person activating an old wound? Am I reacting to him or her like I did my mother or father or some other person who had an impact on me earlier in my life?

- What are five other reasons that could explain their behavior? (Your answers must be reasons other than "because he's stupid, or difficult.")

- Could I allow this person to be difficult or not agree with me and still be okay with myself?

- Can I choose to not react to this person?

- Am I anticipating having my buttons pushed?

- Who or what needs loving understanding in this situation?

TAKE ACTION

Pick one person who pushes your button and ask yourself the questions above and then pick an action step below.

- Let go of an unfair comparison to another person.

- List some other possible reasons for their behavior. Consider them with empathy and compassion.

- Imagine you have an energy shield or filter around you when you are with this person (think "shields up" like in Star Trek), and let what they say and do bounce off.

- Practice "Agree to Disagree" and "Live and Let Live."

- Decide what you are going to do based on what is right, knowing you can handle any possible reaction that may occur.

- Have a difficult conversation and resolve to listen to the other person, trying to discover what they want and need. You may find out important information that changes the feelings you have been having.

REPEATABLE

They can push a
button, but the
response is up to me.

QUESTION 7:
DO I HAVE UNREALISTIC EXPECTATIONS?

"Peace begins when expectations end."
Sri Chinmoy

Sometimes we have unrealistic expectations. Do you expect yourself or others to never make mistakes or have a bad day? Do you expect yourself to be superwoman? Do you expect the best-case scenario will always happen and are you unprepared for those little snags in life?

Karen: When I was in my corporate accounting job, I made myself crazy because I didn't believe it was okay for me to make a mistake. I was much more understanding when my staff members and co-workers made honest mistakes. I'd quickly help them focus on how they could learn from those mistakes and not repeat them. I would encourage them to focus on "Progress, not Perfection." But me? I'd beat myself up over and over again because I was supposed to maintain a higher and truly impossible perfect standard. I had to learn and am still learning to be kinder to myself when I make a mistake. I am human after all!

As a human being, you WILL make mistakes. Can you accept you are human? Can you find the humor in your expectations of yourself and others? Create a healthy attitude about your humanity and develop healthy ways of dealing with those glitches when they happen.

Carol: When I started my own business I thought, "Now I'm going to be my own boss and things will get better. I'll have more control over my time." In fact, for a time things got worse. I found myself thinking about business all the time unable to turn my "inner boss" off. I joked I was the worst boss I have ever had because my expectations were so high. It was harder to delegate in my own business than it ever was in my legal career because I knew exactly how I wanted everything done. I still catch myself doing this. Friends now joke with me when they see me being the "mean boss" and say, "Carol, tell your mean boss you deserve a day off!"

Do you expect others to be mind readers or do things exactly the way you would? Have you caught yourself redoing other people's work because while it was "good enough" it wasn't done the way you would do it? Have you ever said the infamous, "If they loved me, I wouldn't have to tell them what I want or need." WOW. Let's state what we are expecting when we say that, "If they love me, they will develop their mind reader powers to the level so they can read my every desire!" It becomes clear we are placing an unrealistic expectation upon someone we love! Unrealistic expectations such as these inevitably cause disappointment and stress.

You may be trying to live up to all the rules you have adopted or set for yourself. You may think failing is not an option. The way you were raised might have made you ashamed of making mistakes. What if you connected with the innocent and perfect child you were when you entered the world? What if you saw that same innocence in others when they make mistakes or don't live up to what you expected?

Are your expectations aligned with love? If they are not, what would love have you do?

CHECK IN

Take a few minutes and notice the way your expectations add to your stress and keep you from taking action toward the things you desire. Ask yourself the following questions:

- Imagine you wrote a job description of all the things you expect of yourself. Could you hand this job description to another human being and in good conscience expect them to achieve it? Would you ask a friend to take on all that you are telling yourself you have to do? If not, begin to examine the things you'd be willing to take off the job description for someone else and do so for yourself.

- Ask yourself: Will any of this make a difference in a year, ten years or 25 years from now?

- Am I forcing others to adopt my style even when in the whole scope of things it isn't important?

- Am I expecting other people to read my mind?

- Have I taken on expectations that I assume others have for me?

- What is one way I could let go of an expectation to make my life easier right now?

TAKE ACTION

Be careful. It is easy to come up with another set of unrealistic expectations here. If you catch yourself saying, "I'll never make unrealistic expectations of myself again," just laugh! Pick one area where you can lighten up on what you expect of yourself or others. You can move on to other areas and do more as you develop this skill.

REPEATABLE

Relax and remember
we are all human.

QUESTION 8:
AM I TRYING TO BE PERFECT?

"Perfectionism doesn't believe in practice shots. It doesn't believe in improvement. Perfectionism has never heard that anything worth doing is worth doing badly--and that if we allow ourselves to do something badly we might in time become quite good at it. Perfectionism measures our beginner's work against the finished work of masters. Perfectionism thrives on comparison and competition. It doesn't know how to say, 'Good try,' or 'Job well done.' The critic does not believe in creative glee--or any glee at all, for that matter. No, perfectionism is a serious matter." Julia Cameron

When we are in the grip of perfectionism, we tend to make simple things complicated and we judge ourselves and others harshly. This is part of unrealistic expectations but it so affects our lives that we had to give it a category all of its own. Perfection in our human world is a mirage.

Certain tasks require a higher level of commitment to excellence than others do. We all want our physician or airline pilots committed to excellence. Even in those professions, they have to deal with imperfections or change-of-plan scenarios. Pilots who get all passengers safely from point A to point B sometimes experience bumpy flights and landings. Physicians have moments where despite their best efforts; they cannot find a solution for a patient's suffering.

Carol: When I was an actor, I was fit, muscular and curvy. I worked out 2.5 hours a day, at least 5 days a week. I watched what I ate. I wore a size 4, 6 or 8 depending on the clothing. All the messages I got within the acting world were that I was overweight—even though I wasn't. I was right where I should be—even perhaps a little thin for my body type. I remember driving to an audition for a snack product where I was supposed to be a "mom with kids on the beach." "Wear a swimsuit with a skirt or pair of shorts over it in case they want to see your body," my agent told me. I put on self-tanner so my legs weren't white, stressed over what swimsuit to wear, did my hair and makeup and drove the hour across Los Angeles to go to the audition. The closer I got to the studio where the audition was being held, the more my stomach cramped and my palms sweated, "I am not thin enough for this role. I am not perfect enough for the role." I turned around and drove home. Later I saw the advertisement. The woman they chose was probably 30 pounds overweight, and she was beautiful! I might have not gotten the role because I wasn't heavy enough. You could never tell why one actor got a role and another didn't. There was no formula in that world for success. I didn't show up for the audition because of the false idea that I hadn't achieved the perfect body.

Fast forward many years and I am now in my 50s. I am working hard to lose weight and it doesn't come off as easy as it used to. I look back at the pictures of my 28-year-old actor self and say, "Who told you young lady you were fat and not pretty enough? They were wrong!" It still is a struggle for me. The voice that nagged at me as an actor is still there, which is why this question, "Am I trying to be perfect?" is important for me. Fortunately today another voice is present too. It says, "Am I going to let my own or someone else's idea of perfection keep me from living my life? Am I going to not record the video to help people, or do a speaking engagement because I think I have to be perfect before I do it? Am I going to avoid the pool party?"

Trying to be perfect isn't helpful. Taking care of myself, eating well, exercising, etc. is always good for me. Living my life is a blessing--no matter where I am in my fitness regime. I will most likely never live up to my idea of perfection. I will make mistakes, I will have wrinkles and none of that means I am bad. It just means I am human. And that is okay.

If you think what you do has to be a perfect "10" or you must not put your work out there until it is perfect, you are setting yourself up to be unhappy. Karen and I actually had to say to ourselves repeatedly with this project, "Done is better than perfect," otherwise you probably wouldn't be holding this book in your hands. In fact, the book was delayed by several years while we thought we needed to polish and look for better stories to illustrate our points. One evening we sat down and read what we had and we had to say, "Enough! It is good enough!"

If you are always expecting yourself to get straight As in areas that are not important in the overall scope of your life, perhaps it is time to give yourself a break. Sometimes "average" work is good enough!

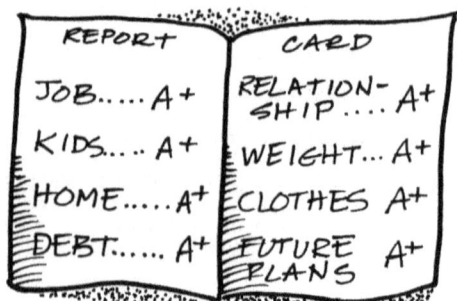

Karen: For years, I have always wanted to do more art. Yet, over and over again, I have not finished projects or not even started some, mainly because I have felt inadequate or that I couldn't get it to come out the way I envisioned it in my head. Now I remind myself the practice of the art is what matters. If I show up for the practice, and detach from outcome, I enjoy the art more.

When we show up for the enjoyment of an event, other people or simply for the joy of doing something we like, creative ideas and outcomes seem to appear or channel through us. We do not have to force ourselves to perform to perfection if we are letting the art appear.

Sometimes the little imperfections turn into "happy accidents" that make something truly beautiful. The Japanese have a phrase called Wabi Sabi, which is about realizing the beauty of things imperfect, impermanent, and incomplete. It is something we can train our mind to start to notice. Take a walk in nature, look at trees, and notice how amazing they are in all their crooked limbs. Notice the beauty in a dying flower. See how many things that at first glance seem "imperfect" are actually quite beautiful. Take a look at Carol's A Shaman on the Walk page on Facebook if you want to see some photographic evidence of this.

Do you link loving yourself to a carefully constructed view of who you have to be and what you have to achieve? Can you believe you are worthy and deserving of love just as you are? We use perfectionist thinking to tell ourselves we aren't THERE yet, rather than recognizing our inherent worth.

Connect with your spiritual perfection rather than your humanly perfection. When you hold a newborn baby, there is a sense of the perfection of life. We don't lose perfection as we grow up; we simply forget that it is there. Take a moment to know you are the same beautiful essence that was born into this world and none of your mistakes diminish who you are.

Much of what you have considered your imperfections and shortcomings may indeed be beautiful, quirky, special and uniquely you. Your very imperfectness is actually perfect just the way it is.

CHECK IN

Ask yourself the following questions:

- Where in your life are you expecting perfection when "good enough" will do?

- Ask yourself if you would be willing to do "C" work in some cases, when you might have expected yourself to turn in an "A" result in the past.

- Consider: Doing your best is possible, whereas perfection is not.

- Where can you let go of an impossible standard you hold for yourself?

- Can you find the Wabi Sabi or beauty in your own and others' imperfections?

- Can you "show up for the practice" and let the outcome flow through?

TAKE ACTION

Let something slide and see what happens.

- Can you clean only half the house each week?

- Can you skip a meeting or send someone else?

- Do you really need to fold all your socks tonight?

- Can you embrace one thing about yourself that you perhaps have judged in the past and love the beauty of that imperfection?

Pick one task or area of your life and experiment with NOT being perfect.

REPEATABLE

Sometimes **DONE** is
better than
PERFECT.

QUESTION 9:
CAN I SAY NO?

"Half of the troubles of this life can be traced to saying yes too quickly and not saying no soon enough." Josh Billings

Do you find yourself saying "Yes" when you know you should say "No"? Are you an expert at managing your time but not living much of a life?

Our modern age seems to value being busy; in fact sometimes being busy turns into a contest. Often that same busyness can make us resentful and tired.

Karen: A women who volunteers for a number of organizations in my community was being introduced by her son at an event. He described her as having "helium arm," and went on to explain whenever anyone needs a volunteer for a task, her arm flies up into the air even before she has time to think about it.

He was being funny, but it got me to thinking about my own fairly acute case of "helium arm." I sometimes volunteer for or agree to do things I do not have time for. There are so many valuable things to be involved with that I hate not to help. I often think I should do something because I know I can do it well. This may be true or untrue, but it is not the best criteria upon which to take on a significant commitment. When we make all our commitments based on what we should do, there is little time to do the things that will make our lives happy and fulfilled.

Even children these days can be so scheduled with activities there is no family downtime. If you are a mom reading this, you may want to look at your children's activities and consider what would happen if you created more free time for the family.

Obviously there are times when you choose to say "yes" to a boss or client or family member when you would prefer to do something else. Part of being an adult is doing the things we may not feel like doing, like going to work on a Monday morning. However, it is important to know what things are essential and when you can say "no." Saying "yes" when you would rather be saying "no" can cause resentment and stress. You end up with more things on your calendar than you can handle. You send a message to yourself that your needs, wishes and desires have no importance. There is also no room for you to say "yes" to the things that might enrich your life or are more aligned with your goals if your calendar is already booked.

This may be one of your biggest challenges. In the beginning, saying "no" instead of your habitual "yes" or "okay" may feel uncomfortable. The more you practice, the easier it will become. Saying "no" reduces the stress of all those extra things you take on and end up resenting.

HOW TO SAY NO. Repeat after us: **NO!**

Okay maybe you are thinking "It isn't that simple." But it is. As Anne Lamott says, "'No' is a complete sentence." When you need to say no, remember the word—it is simple and it is only two letters. You don't have to be mean. An honest, calm and polite "no" is sufficient. Even if the other person tries to convince you, a firm but polite "no" will almost always work. People are happier to accept an honest no, than be faced with indecision and a delayed refusal. Make sure your "yes" means yes and your "no" means no.

The only way to be comfortable saying "no" is to practice. Start with something small and work up to the "nos" you find most difficult.

Be DIRECT. The simple NO

When someone asks you to do something that, you don't want to or can't do, simply say, "No." It is a complete sentence.

> Can you help me with this?

> No.

Okay that may feel a little blunt. It made us burst into laughter when we thought about how abrupt it sounds in comparison to how we normally speak in conversion. You might want to phrase your no with a little more finesse as we will discuss below but the first step in saying no is to know what you want. The second is to have the conviction that you have the right to say, "No" in the same way you have been habitually saying, "Yes." Sometimes there is a place for the simple, direct, "No."

Carol: I took an amazing self-defense course many years ago and one of the first things they taught me in that class was to scream, "NO!" loudly the first moment of any altercation because it would activate my response that it was okay to fight for your life. It often would startle any assailant that might have pegged me for an easy target. Interesting learning to say, "No!" in this self-defense class helped me say, "No," in many other areas of my life.

Most of the places you need to say "no" in life are not as dramatic as being accosted by an assailant. When you remember that you do have that right to a strong internal "no" for anything that does not feel right for you, you are claiming your personal power. You do not have to be talked into another volunteer committee or a piece of cake that isn't on your eating plan.

When you have always said yes, it may take several nos for people to hear you. Repeat the simple statement of refusal again and again. Be clear with yourself that there is no negotiation. Your "no" means NO. No explanation, just repeat it. It's necessary to use this with particularly persistent requests:

No, I can't help you with that project today.

Oh, please, it won't take long.

No, I have other priorities. I won't be able to help you with that project today.

Oh, come on, you are the best at this sort of work.

I appreciate the compliment. However, it doesn't work for me today. Therefore, my answer is still no; I can't help you with that project today.

If someone doesn't take your "no" for an answer after several "nos", they are trying to control you. It's perfectly acceptable at that point to say, "I've told you NO several times. I need you to hear it."

Do these feel a little harsh to you? You don't always have to explain why you can't or do not want to do something. It is your right to say, "No." Perhaps you'd like some examples of how to say, "No," that feel a little more compassionate.

You can express understanding and still say NO. To do this you acknowledge the content and feeling of the request, and then you add the assertive refusal at the end:

I know you want me to help you with the project, and it won't work today. I can't help.

You can give a brief and genuine reason for the refusal without opening up further negotiation:

I can't help you with the project today because I have a report that needs to be finished by tomorrow.

I can't help you today because I have another high-priority commitment.

The other person may still try to persuade you. Often once we start giving "reasons" others may feel it is an invitation to negotiate. You have the right to stand your ground. After you state your reason you may have to go back to a firm, "NO!" to remind yourself (and them) this is not a negotiation. Your no still means no.

You can give them a rain check NO. This is a way of saying that, "No" is a prelude to negotiation, not a rejection of the request. Only use it if you genuinely want to meet the request:

> I can't help you with the project today, but I could help sometime next week.

You can buy yourself some time. Delaying can be a good tactic when you know your tendency is to say, "Yes," too often. Give yourself some time to think about whether you want to take on the project, go out to dinner or whatever other opportunity is being presented

> "I don't know whether it will work for me. Can I check (my calendar, my other commitments etc.) and get back to you?"

Sometimes you need a moment to think away from the person who is asking and you don't have to answer every request in the moment. As a person of integrity, do get back to the requestor. Do not be passive/aggressive and ask for time and then never give an answer. It is not cool to leave others hanging!

If you are still afraid to say, "No," you might need to work on releasing the need to please everyone all the time. You might also want to ask if saying, "Yes," to requests is preventing you from getting to things that your heart is calling you to do. Sometimes we fill up our lives with lots of busy work so we don't have to take the leap into the important things that scare us.

Your soul may be longing for space in your schedule for you to slow down, take time to evaluate what is important to you, add some self-care activities or perhaps to do nothing at all. You won't know until you clear out some space to listen to what you your heart and soul want. They tend to speak in whispers rather than shouts.

Do you fear if you create space for yourself that everything will fall apart? The opposite is true. You create the emotional space and time to do what you choose to do. It also allows space and time for new things to come into your life, some of which you would have never noticed managing a wall-to-wall schedule.

Can you imagine clearing some time for you simply to have a few moments each day or each week with nothing on your calendar? How would that feel?

Carol: I remember a holiday weekend we all were going to be working at my law firm job. We decided to have a potluck since the restaurants near the office building were all going to be closed for the holiday. My co-workers asked me to bring my lasagna, which I always made from scratch. Part of me was thinking in that moment, "Am I going to have time with work and other commitments to make lasagna?" I didn't say, "No," and I found myself up till 2 a.m. the night before the potluck, making the lasagna. When I arrived at work, another co-worker of mine, Peggy said she had been outside until midnight barbequing the chicken she had promised to bring. We commiserated with each other. Then co-worker after co-worker walked in with things from the grocery store saying, "I know I promised to make my homemade potato salad but I didn't have time." Peggy and I looked at each other and laughed because when we had said yes it never occurred to us we could change our minds or not bring the homemade dish. I could have said, "I am not sure whether I'll have time for the homemade version, but I promise I'll bring something." Since I had a hard time saying no to bringing a homemade potluck dish, you can imagine all the places where not being able to say no got me into trouble in my life and caused me immense stress.

People often compliment me about how clear my boundaries are and there is no doubt my "no" means NO. This wasn't a skill I was born with. It took many years for me to be comfortable saying no with grace. In the beginning I think I came across as a little aggressive because I so need to be emphatic to remind myself it was okay for me to say, "No." I know when I am loving and clear, my life works better. There is a balance between wanting to help people, pitching in and helping the committee run and taking on too much. I have to assess where I need to say no more. I also need to remember if I am certain of my yeses and nos, others will respect what I say. They may not be happy but I am not responsible for their happiness, only for being clear about what I am willing to do.

If you have been someone who always says, "Yes," learning to say, "No," takes practice.

If you have already said, "Yes," when you should have said, "No," you will have to weigh whether this is a learning experience for you to keep your commitment this time and remember to be stronger with your "no" in the future; or if you need to go back and clean up the too hasty "yes." You can renegotiate your commitments.

Karen: A few years back I agreed to be the membership chair for a women's organization I was involved with. I did the job for a year during the presidency of a very good friend. The next president asked if I would continue, and without thinking it through, I said, "Sure!" It was a pretty fun job (but lots of work), I had done a good job (with lots of work), and I liked feeling needed (and it was lots of work). When I finally sat down to think about the year ahead, I realized I had been doing the position mainly as a favor to my friend, and I was not willing to do it any longer. I had to go through the uncomfortable experience of telling the new president I had changed my mind, but I felt so relieved after I did. A weight had been lifted.

As I wrote about this example, I thought of at least five other times in the past several years where I had become enrolled in someone else's dream or idea, and signed on to help or be a partner. There was the jewelry company, the skincare company, the networking group board position, the coaching idea, and the health supplement company. In every case, I probably should have said, "No," but I hate to be left out, and I get excited about new ideas. In each case, the work involved was not on the path to my dreams or in fulfillment of my ideas. I then had to extricate myself. While I can say that I have gained something from every experience, I also learned to consider whether a project, event, or idea is good for me before I jump in with both feet. The biggest learning is that I can say, "No," even after the fact if I made a mistake, and it doesn't make me a bad person.

CHECK IN

Think about the things you have committed to recently and ask yourself:

- Where have I said, "Yes," lately when I should have said, "No"?

- Who do I find it hard to say, "No," to?

- Why am I saying, "Yes"? Is it a good reason for me?

- How much of my stress comes from not saying, "No"?

- Can I renegotiate my commitments?

- Can I change my mind about doing some things?

TAKE ACTION

Look at your schedule today. Is there is something that could be a "no" instead of a "yes?" Where have you been automatically saying, "Yes," where a clear, "No," would be better?

- Pick one thing to say, "No," to today. The more you practice saying, "No," the easier you will find it to do.

- Renegotiate something that you already committed to. Lessen your involvement or back out graciously if you should not have said, "Yes," in the first place.

- Schedule some open time on your calendar. Even if it is only five to ten minutes a day.

- Check in and see whether your yeses and nos are aligned with a life you choose or whether you are so caught up in saying yes to everything that you are running on autopilot with no time for what you truly desire.

REPEATABLE

I have the right to say NO.

QUESTION 10:
WHAT AM I JUGGLING?

"Juggling is an illusion. ... In reality, the balls are being independently caught and thrown in rapid succession. ... It is actually task switching." Gary Keller

Most of us have competing demands on our time, and often we manage it all well. But each new day, and sometimes each hour in a day, things occur that make us have to reassess all the things we are juggling: Work, family, friends, spiritual time, fun time, etc. Over-commitment is the natural outcome of not saying NO and adding more and more to our juggling routines. If you are good at juggling, others may keep throwing you more balls. You may find yourself struggling to find that illusive balance we hear so much about. As though balance is a place that you can go to and once you have arrived, you are set for life.

Balance, if it exists, is the ability to be constantly flexible and flow with the changing demands. It is about knowing whether everything you are juggling needs your attention. Life constantly presents opportunities to choose what is most important.

We also have to assess what we are juggling with both short-term and long-term vision. If work is constantly handing you crisis projects, there may come a time when you realize that your focus needs to be on the other areas of your life you keep setting aside for work. Our relationships, our health, and our spiritual connection can be neglected for a short period of time to finish a project but if we neglect them for too long the damage can be hard to repair.

It is important to notice how our decisions impact all the areas of our life. Sometimes we are stressed because we have to make tough decisions.

Karen: I have had to work hard on this in conjunction with the over-commitment tendency we talked about in the previous chapter. A few years back, I realized I was loading up my "To Do" list with lots of tasks that did not advance my dreams and goals, but which would allow me to feel better about my accomplishments and productivity. If I put many small tasks on the list to juggle, and then did them, I could check off lots more things on my long list and I got to feel better about getting things done. However, some of the things that I needed to dig into–things that would have helped me make more money or change my circumstances never got started. I was using my ability to juggle lots of tasks to procrastinate and avoid doing some big things. I started asking myself whether something even needed to be listed, and then whether it was the most important thing to work on this day. A hint here: If you find yourself cleaning out your underwear drawer when you should be tackling your taxes, you may be in the same boat I was.

Carol: I've always been a "doer." I love having multiple projects going at once. I love being busy. I love solving problems. For a good portion of my adult life I have worked in corporate America in one capacity or another to fund my passion projects—acting, writing and exploration of mystical and spiritual traditions. I would schedule myself from early in the morning until late at night bouncing between "money jobs" to passion projects.

The first time someone told me to slow down with that often repeated phrase, "We are human beings, not human doings," it didn't resonate with me at all, because my self-worth was intricately tied to the things I did. I was proud when people would say to me, "I don't know how you DO all you do." I wore my busyness like a badge of honor.

The problem with this was I would go on like this for months on end until I was overtired, resentful and often times physically ill. I was very susceptible to colds. I made a commitment to schedule some time to do nothing at all. This led to time meditating. If you've read my first book *From Scared to Sacred* you'll know meditating didn't come easily for me. My doer simply didn't want to sit still. Slow-down time is exactly what my busy self needs. I can make better decisions about what is important to me when I have those moments to breathe.

When I wrote *From Scared to Sacred,* I committed to listening to Spirit and writing an hour a day. Many days I had to determine what was going to be set aside so I could keep that promise. Sometimes I shorted myself on sleep so I had the extra hour to write. For a period of time, I did little other than write for weeks on end. I went into a cave, and didn't have much social life. I was fine with those choices during the most intense part of channeling the book but when it came time to work on the polishing and crafting of the prose, I readjusted the priorities to feel whole again. I reconnected with friends, recommitted to exercise and rest, and found more time for play.

Sometimes we focus so much on doing the things we are juggling we forget about how we want to *be* in the world. We need quiet moments to make sure we haven't lost a connection to something important in our lives. You don't decide your priorities once and have everything work perfectly; you need to reassess periodically and see if what you are juggling today are the important things to you.

CHECK IN

Take a few minutes now to notice all the things you are juggling.

- What are all the competing demands for your attention?

- Have you been neglecting an important area of your life?

- Are you doing something now or planning to do something that could be done later?

- Have you accurately assessed your priorities?

- Are you working on the thing that is most important right now?

- Should you be DOING or would the best thing to be to put down all the balls and give yourself some quiet time to BE?

- What is the hard call you need to make right now to make sure the important things are being handled?

- What are you juggling that does not need to be on your list, at least not right now?

TAKE ACTION

- Depending on your answers above, pick one or two things you might release to simplify your current juggling routine.
- Notice if something important needs to be picked up and attend to the relationship or activity.

REPEATABLE

It doesn't all have
to be done now.
Maybe it doesn't
have to be
done at all!

QUESTION 11:
AM I THE QUEEN OF MULTI-TASKING?

"There's no such thing as multitasking."
Jim Loehr

Even when we make sure we are only juggling the important things, we can be caught up in the myth of the power of multitasking. Multitasking often comes easily to women. It is part of the evolutionary process. Women in general are better multitaskers because of our traditional need to tend to the children, and take care of all the other things in the home at the same time. But here is a big blow to all of us who think we are great multitaskers: it can diminish our efficiency and ability to be present with a specific task, or with other people.

The truth is there is no such thing as doing more than one thing at a time. What master multi-taskers do is switch very rapidly between objects of attention (tasks) back and forth in their minds. Those of us who are proud of our ability to multi-task believe we are in control of what we are switching back and forth between, and we think it allows us to get much more done.

There are big downsides to constant multi-tasking. The mind must determine where it left off every time it switches between tasks. No matter how fast it does this, it is not as effective as if we had given our full attention to one task for even a short while longer. When we are distracted by thoughts of two or more things, we are not doing our best on the task at hand. We may miss important details, minimize issues or risks in situations, skip over important steps, not hear what someone says, and miss opportunities to be fully present with another human being.

A study conducted by the U.S. Federal Aviation Administration, cited in American Psychology Association Online[5] showed that time lags when switching between tasks were greater when the tasks were more complex, and when the tasks were less familiar to the person. They identified two distinct steps occur in the brain whenever we switch tasks: "goal shifting ("I want to do this now instead of that.")" and "rule activation ("I'm turning off the rules for that and turning on the rules for this.")." These steps take several tenths of a second, which can add up when you switch repeatedly. This time lag can be great enough in some circumstances to create danger. The article points out "a mere half second of time lost to task switching can mean the difference between life and death for a driver using a cell phone, because during the time that the car is not totally under control, it can travel far enough to crash into obstacles the driver might have otherwise avoided."

---

[5]Found at: http://www.apa.org/releases/multitasking.html.

Constant multitasking also keeps us from practicing the spiritual principle of PRESENCE: being fully in this moment and with the actual human beings we share our lives with. Perhaps it is time to take the multi-tasking crown off and simply *be* in this moment!

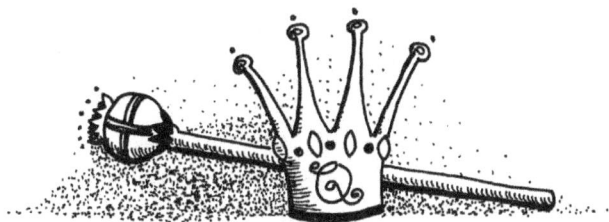

Karen: When my oldest son graduated from high school I was definitely the Queen of Multi-Tasking. I was organizing the celebration of this important event, along with getting him to choose a college, planning summer activities, finishing home school with my 13-year-old, and working.

Fortunately, I did stop doing long enough to be present and experience several never to be forgotten moments and feelings. Things do not fall apart if they aren't done how I envisioned or on the schedule I originally set. As I navigated that busy time, I noticed I was moving so fast from task to task, I was in danger of blowing right through the very moments I was doing so much for. I also became aware I was avoiding feelings I knew I didn't want to face. As I slowed down and focused on my feelings about all I had been doing, and about my son graduating and leaving the nest, my feelings went through a broad spectrum: numbness and fatigue ("I just have to get through all these events!"), impatience and resentment ("Why am I doing everything?"), worry and regret ("What if we didn't do enough these past 18 years?"), sadness ("How can 18 years be over already? My baby is going away!") to an incredible sense of pride and awe at what my son has accomplished and become. I could then be present with him and the rest of our family in a place of joy. It still makes me feel a bit choked up thinking of it all, nine years later.

Being in the moment had great benefits. I clearly experienced the beautiful sunset light and the excitement in the air at the graduation (the first ever at his high school), the love of friends and family who surrounded us, and the look on my son's face when he got an unexpected award. I am so very glad to have changed focus and stopped thinking about things like the seating chart for the celebration dinner.

Carol: I can multitask and do it well but to be my most productive, I need to narrow my focus, close the door, turn off my phone, and work. This is what allowed me to become an author. I find it sad that so many of us are walking around not fully present and buying into the myth that multi-tasking is better. I think I can check in with a friend while I finish paying my bills on my computer. Problem is there are times when I have to do a bit of math and I stop listening to my friend. Taking a walk, I see a woman pushing a baby in a stroller but talking on the phone and missing the opportunity to talk with her child and point things out as they walk. In a restaurant, waiting for a friend, I observe how many tables of people have their phones out and are texting or checking information on their phones.

I have made a commitment to try to stop multitasking whenever I can. Just because someone sends a text, email or leaves a voicemail message, does not mean I have to switch what I am doing to respond immediately. I leave my phone in my purse when I'm out to lunch or dinner with someone unless there is a pressing call I am waiting for and then I tell the person I'm with why my phone is on the table. Presence with friends and family is so important. Not surprisingly, my stress levels have gone down as I focus on taking one thing at a time.

CHECK IN

- Do you consider yourself to be a master at multi-tasking?

- Do you find yourself working on more than one thing at once?

- Do you continue to type memos or organize papers while taking a phone call?

- Do you keep working and sometimes not look at a person who comes into your office, while you are having a conversation with them?

- Do you do things while driving (talk on the phone, eat, do your makeup, read the paper)?

- Do you sometimes feel you have so many projects open on your desk or your computer that you forget where you are?

- Do you answer the phone every time it rings, even if you are in the middle of a conversation or task?

- Have you missed what someone important was saying or not noticed something going on because you were so busy with several other tasks or details?

- How might all this multi-tasking be contributing to your feelings of overwhelm or stress?

TAKE ACTION

The key to breaking this pattern is to slow down and be mindful. Try one or two of the following actions today to help yourself to do this. Start small. Even a few minutes of actual concentration can make a difference.

- Concentrate on one thing at a time and give it your full attention.

- Deliberately listen on a phone call and do nothing else but take notes on what is being said. Seek to understand and clarify what you hear rather than rushing to respond.

- Put everything aside when someone comes into your office, look them in the eye, and give them your full attention. Listen to more than their words.

- Set time aside in your schedule for specific projects, and allow yourself to work only on one thing during that time.

- Close your door for even a short period of time, and do not answer your phone while you do your project or write a memo.

- Take a moment to notice what is going on around you. What are you missing by being absorbed by your tasks?

REPEATABLE

Just do one thing
at a time.

QUESTION 12:
AM I LAST ON MY LIST?

"Rest and self-care are so important. When you take time to replenish your spirit, it allows you to serve others from the overflow. You cannot serve from an empty vessel."

Eleanor Brownn

Self-care is often the thing we neglect in the DOING of our lives. Is your health and well-being on your priority list? Do you think making you a priority or taking time for yourself is selfish? If you don't have health and energy, how can you function? If you are so overwhelmed with conflicting values between work and home, how do you focus on doing your job well? In addition, what is the ultimate toll on your relationships and personal life?

One of the first rules of first aid is to clearly assess the situation and not put yourself in more danger when rescuing someone so you avoid having two victims. Every time you fly, the flight attendant makes that announcement—you know the one you don't pay any attention to anymore about the oxygen masks—

put on your mask first and then assist others. We are sure you've heard this analogy before but we want to ask you to contemplate a fundamental question: Do you even get a mask in your current life? Where are you in the lineup of priorities?

Carol: I have had to pay particular attention to a pattern of pushing myself so hard to meet others and my own tough expectations. I get much satisfaction from being the rescuer— the one who swoops in and saves the day by staying up until two in the morning to finish a project.

Many times, I would work so hard until my body would shut down and I would need to spend all day Sunday in bed. If I didn't, I would end up sick.

All my upbringing was about putting others first. To change this pattern, I had to reach back into my Catholic school upbringing to ask myself this question: "If the great commandment was to love God and love our neighbor as ourselves, and I'm not doing a good job of loving myself, how much is there of me to truly love others?"

Karen: This one is particularly ironic for me, since I own a day spa and my husband is a massage therapist. Yet as I wrote this, I realized I had not had a massage or a facial in over two months, despite the easy availability. I had again put many other things before my well-being, and my back was definitely telling me so. Here again was my chance to live by what I tell my clients when

I urge them to allow themselves the care they would wish for everyone else in their lives.

So many women we know aren't even on their own list of things to take care of. And eventually this takes a toll. Karen has a friend whose mother was consumed by taking care of her husband who was dying of cancer. She had several symptoms she ignored, and after her husband died, she finally went to the doctor. The mother's symptoms turned out to be her own cancer, which had spread so much there was nothing to be done except keep her comfortable. She had delayed too long. We could say that perhaps she had a soul contract to not live long after her husband, but there was also a lesson for all who heard about it. It is important to listen to your body, follow your intuition, and take care of yourself.

So we ask you this important question: "What is the most loving way to take care of yourself?"

CHECK IN

Some questions to ask yourself:

- Have I taken care of my basic bodily needs? (Thirst, hunger, restroom, breathing, etc.)

- Can I do something to relax my body? (Stretch, walk around the block, change my position at my desk?)

- Would anything bad happen if I took a break right now?

- Have I forgotten to do the things I know will help me?

- Can I share what I am feeling with someone? Can I talk to someone about it?

- Can I turn to my spiritual beliefs to help me in this situation?

TAKE ACTION

Schedule one thing that takes care of you in the next week.

- What is one thing you could do to take better care of yourself: your health, your mind, your spirit?

- Find a small way you can take care of yourself. Even if you only have a few minutes to breathe and stretch, take a time out to give yourself the message, "I care about you and will take care of you."

- You can start small. Pick one thing you know will help you feel better emotionally or physically. Make a commitment to take care of yourself so that you can take care of all the other things you are juggling in your life.

REPEATABLE

Regular self-care is essential.

QUESTION 13:
AM I ASKING FOR WHAT I NEED?

"The number one reason that we don't get our needs met, we don't express them. We express judgments. If we do express needs, the number two reason we don't [get] our needs met, [is] we don't make clear requests." Marshall Rosenberg[6]

There are many people who go through life thinking they have to do it all themselves. Some of this comes from the curse of perfectionism but for others it comes from not asking for help when they need it. If you feel like you have to do everything yourself and you can't delegate or ask others to help you, you may be increasing your stress load and be unable to access the power of working with others to increase your effectiveness.

You also may be walking through the world sending an unconscious message that you like to go it alone and you don't

---

[6] We've modified this quote for sense as the ways we've seen it recorded are obviously missing words.

need any help. If you are one of those super competent people, you may find others saying things to you like, "I would have asked if you needed help but you looked like you had it under control."

Carol: Oh, do I relate to this one! I was raised to be self-sufficient and be the one who helps others. I'd often find myself tired and resentful at having to do it all myself. Moreover, I often asked for help in a manner that sounded like I could do it myself if the person I asked could not help me. I once found myself moving my whole apartment by myself because I kept telling people, "If you could help me I'd appreciate it, but I'll be okay if you can't." I wasn't okay! Even with the two movers I had hired to move the heavy stuff, I was exhausted and teary by the end of the day. I kicked myself for making it seem like I did not need help.

Karen: I clearly recall having a similar breakdown point. I was always the person who helped others solve their problems, think through issues, and feel better. No wonder I became a Hypnotherapist. I remember clearly thinking, "Why is it no one does this for me?" The answer was I seldom let down my guard about my own issues with my friends, and I almost never asked for help or even a helpful ear. To this day, I still have to work on this one. My signal it is happening again is when I start to feel resentment. I now know enough to say to myself, "Stop being such a martyr!"

In a spiritual sense, we all take on different archetypes at different times in life. Many women have a version of being a martyr (what Carol and I were doing), being a heroine or rescuer (swooping in to help or take care of others), or even being a prostitute (giving up parts of yourself to satisfy another or get something you want). None of these roles is inherently bad or wrong. It is simply useful to notice whether you are acting in one of them to your detriment.

There are many times in life when we need assistance or emotional support. No one is an island. You may be good at giving to others but your receiving muscles may be atrophied. You may need to practice asking for help.

CHECK IN

- Am I someone who has a hard time delegating projects or asking for assistance?

- Do I think I have to do it all myself?

- Do I get mad or feel resentment because I have to do it all myself and no one helps me?

- Have I asked anyone for assistance in the last month?

- Have I been willing to seek out someone with more experience in this area to mentor me?

- Do I start every project as though no one else has done it before or am I comfortable looking for expert advice or using what others have done before?

- Do I ask for a hug or someone to listen to me when I need it?

- Do I even know what I need?

TAKE ACTION

Look for one thing you could ask for help with and ask someone for assistance. If the first person says no, ask someone else.

REPEATABLE

Help is there for the asking. I am willing to receive it.

QUESTION 14:
AM I HONORING MY FEELINGS?

"Feelings like disappointment, embarrassment, irritation, resentment, anger, jealousy,
and fear, instead of being bad news, are
actually very clear moments that teach us
where it is that we're holding back. They
teach us to perk up and lean in when we feel
we'd rather collapse and back away. They're
like messengers that show us, with terrifying
clarity, exactly where we're stuck. This very
moment is the perfect teacher, and, lucky for
us, it's with us wherever we are."

Pema Chodron

Events in life can stir up intense or uncomfortable feelings and
often times we choose not to express those feelings in the
moment. Your boss takes credit for your work. Your client yells
they don't like the service your company has been giving. You
are sad because your child is having a hard time with his or her

105

peers at school. You may not want to blurt out everything you are feeling, but it is important you find a space to honor the emotions present. If you suppress your feelings you may find it feels like you are trying to hold a beach ball under water–it ALWAYS pops out. Often your feelings erupt at the most inopportune time, when you simply no longer have the energy to "hold it together." Or if you are successful at keeping the beach ball submerged, those feelings take a toll on your physical and mental health.

When you are angry, frustrated, sad, or whatever other feeling you are experiencing, NOTICE IT and NAME IT. Do not ignore or cover the emotion over before you have experienced it. Those emotions have important messages for you.

Carol: As someone who values being loving and kind, I have often dismissed my anger or disappointment as not "spiritual" rather than seeing it as a sign a boundary was violated or I had been looking forward to something that didn't work out. I remember one Saturday I was holding a community fire ceremony at my home. I had 15 people RSVP they would attend. As the day wore on and the ceremony drew near, my email and cell phone filled with messages saying some version of, "Sorry I won't be able to make it tonight." Most of the people who couldn't attend had very good reasons for not attending (or at least they made up good reasons for not attending). I was frustrated. I had made a huge pot of soup for 15 and it turned out only one person showed up. I was disappointed because I had a vision of a powerful ceremony with 15 people and that wasn't going to be. As much as I tried to tell myself, "This is perfect and Spirit knows who should be here and it will all work out," I couldn't get past my feelings of having no one I could count on to be there. So before my one friend got there, I sat down and allowed myself to grieve the vision I had for the ceremony and the feeling no one wanted to come to my party. (True or not, that is how I felt.) When I did, I was able to be in a better place and when my one guest arrived, we had a powerful intimate ceremony. It did all work out but I needed to process and let go of the disappointment before I could surrender to what was. And I was able to freeze the soup. It came in handy a few months later when I got a bad cold and didn't feel like cooking.

Karen: Our family is famous for not sharing "real feelings" and for acting like everything is fine when it's not. Looking back, I can recall many times when my mother kept a lid on whatever was going on for her, and sometimes the feelings came out in a totally unrelated arena later on, or became self-directed. "I'm fine!" is a familiar family phrase. I do not recall seeing her cry when her mother died, but I do recall we were yelled at to clean up our rooms. As an adult and mother myself, I have had to own up to my own deep tendencies in this area. After all, I was trained by the best. When my parents got a divorce, I simply resolved not to let that happen to me. When I was frustrated in school or disappointed at work, I worked hard to be positive.

When I was seven months pregnant, we experienced the 1994 Northridge earthquake (after which my home required over $100,000 in repairs). I got up and figured out how to make coffee on the camp stove without a coffee grinder, and then started planning how I would get to work. After all, I was one of the senior managers in inventory control, and, "I would be needed." My husband looked at me like I was crazy. I definitely was in some sort of denial.

This tendency to muffle feelings can be so strong for me that I was surprised to hear my husband's experience of the quake itself. At the time, I remember saying, "Oh, this is like the one we had the other day," despite the fact everything flew off of our nightstands and our dresser fell over and almost hit my husband as he ran to get our son. I experienced it as smaller than it was. On the other hand, Brian heard the wood of our house creaking, the glass breaking, and the rumble of the earth moving—a much more amplified and complete experience. He was still able to function at a high level, and he definitely had more conscious information than I did.

I have noticed the feelings I ignore or bury often burst out later, as they did with my mom. More importantly, if they do not, they make themselves known in other more destructive ways. I eat things I shouldn't and wonder why as I am doing it. I escape into a nap or longer sleep at night. I play games on my phone or read a book instead of getting important tasks done. Or I get chronic heartburn or a certain nagging pain in my neck. The feelings are still there, and will have their say at some point.

As I admit that I have feelings, honor them and let them out, they dissipate. The physical and behavioral signs are clues I have been ignoring important messages, which would be helpful to me if I listen to them.

Even people who express their feelings often don't do the work to truly honor them. Expressing the feelings is only the first step. Honoring your feelings means listening to the messages they are bringing you. For example, there could be many reasons for being angry but simply yelling and expressing anger won't help you understand what the angry feeling is trying to tell you. Do you need to set some boundaries? Are you overdoing it? Do you need to communicate something?

What are your feelings trying to tell you?

CHECK IN

It is good to periodically take your emotional temperature and find healthy, constructive ways to experience and learn from your emotions.

- What are the feelings you haven't had time to process?

- Can you name the feeling or feelings you are having?

- What other symptoms are you experiencing that are clues you may have emotions to listen to?

- Think back to events over the last week where you needed to "muscle through." What feelings did you stuff down?

TAKE ACTION

Here are few ways you can work with your feelings in a healthy way:

- Give them names. Even if you do not know exactly what a feeling is, give it a name that comes closest to what you can describe right now. (Or you could call it that FRED feeling. No offense to Freds in the world. You can use any name that works for you. One of our friends calls these feelings Icky. The name would stand in for the feeling unidentified but deeply felt at this moment.)

- Consider the feeling and ask it what it is trying to communicate to you. Notice what the message of the feeling seems to be.

- Make the feeling a character. Who is it? A gun fighter in the Old West? A damsel in distress? A hurt lion? Notice what information this character can show you.

- Think about the feelings as important visitors. They are there for you, but they are separate from you. You are not your feelings.

- Write in a journal.

- Write a letter to another person and *do not* send it.

- Ask a friend to stand in for the person you need to say something to.

- Punch a pillow.

- Drive somewhere private and scream in your car.

- Write down everything that is bothering you and burn the pieces of paper (safely, please!).

- Rent a movie that will help you cry out a feeling.

REPEATABLE

Feelings are important messengers. Listen to them.

QUESTION 15:
IS THIS EVENT ACTIVATING
OLD WOUNDS?

"You can accept or reject the way you are treated by other people, but until you heal the wounds of your past, you will continue to bleed. You can bandage the bleeding with food, with alcohol, with drugs, with work, with cigarettes, with sex, but eventually, it will all ooze through and stain your life. You must find the strength to open the wounds, stick your hands inside, pull out the core of the pain that is holding you in your past, the memories, and make peace with them."

Iyanla Vanzant

Your experience of the events in your life doesn't happen in a vacuum. Each time something happens, your subconscious goes to work trying to figure out what the event means based on what has happened in your past. It can be helpful to look at what deeper wounds or patterns are being activated, especially when your response to an event feels out of proportion to what happened. Are you re-enacting a karmic wound? Is this event trying to help you heal a relationship or experience from your childhood or a trauma from your past?

Karen: One of my very best friends retired from her job and moved from our community in Southern California to her new home near Austin, Texas. She is now near her son, and back near where she grew up. I totally understand it, I am happy for her, and know I can visit and keep in touch electronically. At the same time, I felt sad and abandoned. I'm not typically a "needy" friend, but I felt like she was leaving me when I needed her most. I also know this is out of proportion and unfair to her. When I examine this, I can trace it back to several "earlier similars" in my life, all the way back to when my friend Melanie moved away in seventh grade to Texas, of all places! We had become such close friends and had lots of adolescent plans for the future, including helping each other write a book. After she moved, I promptly lost touch with her, and I truly regretted that. Then it happened in 11th grade with my new best friend, Nancy–she moved back to Charleston, where she had come from. After a couple more of these, I started to think of myself as "the one who is left to carry on alone" and then, "the one who is bad at keeping in touch."

OH. I REALLY THOUGHT I WAS OVER THAT.

Carol: You can find yourself re-enacting old wounds from your childhood you thought you were long over. I had this experience with a simple car accident. One day, I wasn't paying attention while driving in a parking lot and drove over a curb and ended up ripping the whole front bumper off my car. Accidents happen. I was lucky. I wasn't hurt. No one else was hurt. I didn't damage anyone else's property. But I still felt so stupid and anxious. As I called the insurance company to report my claim because the repair was more than my personal budget could handle, I was so uncomfortable. When I asked myself what I was uncomfortable about, I found I was afraid of being yelled at for making a mistake. My rational mind knew this wasn't likely. My insurance company pays people to take phone calls about claims and I highly doubted the person on the phone would yell. But the fear was there along with anxiety and stress. I pushed myself to move through the discomfort to report the accident but after the phone call I also did something else. I looked deeper and asked, "Where did that feeling of being yelled at for making a mistake come from?" I felt myself traveling back through time to being a little girl spilling my milk at the dinner table and my mom yelling at me for being careless. I remember feeling small and ashamed. I had the same feeling at over 50 years old that I had at 5. I internalized at a very young age I was supposed to try to be perfect, mistakes weren't okay and my worth was tied to being so careful I never make a mistake. What a set up for stress!

We have a huge opportunity for unlocking old subconscious programming when feelings such as these hit you. This is a time we can re-parent our internal child and say, "I know you didn't mean it and you were scared by how upset mom was, but it wasn't about the milk. It was about things going on in your mom's life too." For example, can you imagine the stress it must have been to keep up with the expectations of being a housewife in the 1960s? Can you see how she might have felt like she didn't want to clean up one more mess? I can.

Sometimes simply realizing the stress you are feeling isn't all about what is happening now can help you shift it. Other times you need help to heal those old wounds and patterns so your energy is all here in the present moment.

All the memories we have stored in our subconscious minds create a context through which we look at the world. Many of us are unconsciously looking at our world through filters that are no longer accurate. We might even have some post-traumatic stress from events in our past. Stress is triggered in the new situation that is similar to the old pattern. We may have subconscious stories like, "I'm not good enough," "I am unlovable," or "I never do things right," which cause us to lack confidence to face the challenges in our lives at the moment. If we walk around perceiving we aren't good enough, perhaps the people around us are picking up on that and treating us in a manner reflecting those internal feelings.

As healthy people who function well in the world, we can still have moments where we find it is time to do some work healing those old patterns. Often times this work is best done by collaborating with a therapist or healer. When we practice telling a new story, we shift the energy and free ourselves.

CHECK IN

- What feelings or emotions are you experiencing right now?

- Have you experienced a feeling like this in the past? When?

- What are you telling yourself about you based on those feelings?

- Is an old script coming up that is ready to be changed? ("I am not worthy, "I can never get what I need," etc.)

- How is the current situation different from the past?

- How have you changed and grown since the original past experience?

- What truth can you see about the past you were not equipped to see back then?

- Can you celebrate releasing an old idea about yourself?

- What is another story you can tell about yourself and that old thing?

TAKE ACTION

Write a letter to the previous version of you, acknowledging the hurt or fear. Tell the part of you what you wanted to hear.

If this feels too difficult for you, get some help.

REPEATABLE

An old wound acknowledged and honored unburdens the present and future.

QUESTION 16:
WHAT IS THE NEXT SMALL STEP
I CAN TAKE TODAY?

"A journey of a thousand miles begins with one small step." Chinese Proverb

It can be easy to get overwhelmed when you have big dreams or when life throws you an unexpected curve ball. The scope of a project or life event feels bigger than you can handle. There is so much to do and you don't know where to start. You start thinking things like, "How can I possibly get this all done?" or, "I don't know what to do," or maybe even, "I can't face the world today!"

The answer is most often simply doing the obvious, small thing right in front of you. When you are emotionally overwhelmed or feeling down, the next obvious thing could be something simple like taking a shower or going for a walk. If you are unemployed it might be making one phone call to a contact to ask about potential job openings. If you are dealing with a big work project, it might be sitting down and making a list of all the different things that have to happen and people you need to

119

contact. If you have a big problem you don't know how to fix, it might be seeking out advice from a trusted source.

We reclaim our power when we do the small things we can do now. Once we take the first small step, other steps become clear to us. Even if we take a step and it doesn't work out the way we'd hoped, that step gives us information that can help us determine the next step.

Carol: One of my dear friends, Victorea, was going through some major changes her in life. Recently divorced, she had sold her ranch in Texas thinking she would easily be able to find a property in Kentucky or Tennessee where she wanted to move. She had a herd of cattle, two dogs and a cat to think about in addition to moving a household and farming equipment. As the closing date on her Texas property loomed near, she still had not found a suitable property that fit her needs. I would talk to her each day. She was understandably stressed. What could she do? It became apparent the Universe had a different timing for finding her property than she did. All she could do was take the next step in front of her. Pack her personal belongings. Find temporary pasture space for the cattle. Arrange for movers to pick up her belongings and move them to storage. When she focused on what she could do, the overwhelming feelings diminished slightly. She still had a major move to get through but by focusing on what she could do now, it gave her back her power. I'm happy to report she did eventually find her property and was able to move in with a two-month gap between when she sold her ranch and when she was settled in her new place. When we are overwhelmed, we often need someone to help us break down the simple steps we can do right now rather than the big list of things we will eventually need to do. Victorea has done the same for me many times.

Karen: This happened to me when I came home from the hospital with our first child. I was tired and overwhelmed in a different way than I had ever experienced before. I remember thinking, "If I cannot even take a shower or get dressed before noon, how am I ever going to go back to work?" It felt daunting, and everyone's advice didn't help how I felt. How was I going to get this baby thing down and get back to any semblance of normal life? Thankfully, I had the presence of mind to know millions of other mothers had handled this before me, many in MUCH more challenging circumstances. That thought helped me relax a bit and focus on what was in front of me. Change the baby, use the bathroom, take a shower while he naps, or at night after my husband gets home. If I put him down for a while and got dressed, nothing bad happened. The small steps started to work, and with each one I got more confident and could get more accomplished. About two weeks in, our heater was turned off by the gas company for being unsafe (it was December!) and I broke my toe. For a while, I had to crawl because I could not put any weight on my foot, and the heater took a week to be replaced. I felt the overwhelming and helpless feelings start to come back. But by then I knew I could handle this if I kept doing one thing at a time, and only doing what I could. We set up a room with most of what I would need during the day: a cooler, the phone (no cell phones then!), the TV, some books, all the baby stuff, and a space heater. If I needed anything else, I crawled or hopped to get it while Kyle napped. I couldn't do any cleaning, I didn't get any of the crafts done I hoped I would while out on leave, and no closets got organized. But I could focus on my son who needed to lie in the sun to help clear his jaundice. I could get the breastfeeding routine down. AND I could savor this time I had been given to be there with him. Sometimes events conspire to force you to let some things go and focus in on what truly needs attention. Sometimes chaotic and overwhelming circumstances are a gift.

CHECK IN

If you are feeling overwhelmed or unclear check in and brainstorm:

- What are the possible small actions I can take?

- Who are possible resources I could reach out to?

- What needs to happen next?

- How have you gotten yourself moving in the past?

TAKE ACTION

- Pick one small simple step you can take right now and do it.

REPEATABLE

Take a step-- any step.

QUESTION 17:
WHERE (OR WHO) IS MY TRIBE?

"If you want to accomplish something that demands determination and endurance, try to surround yourself with people possessing these qualities. And try to limit the time you spend with people given to pessimism and expressions of futility. Unfortunately, negative emotions exert a more powerful effect in social situations than positive ones, thanks to the phenomena of emotional contagion." Richard Restak, M.D.

We need social interaction and support and sometimes the hardest thing to find is the tribe made up of people who understand and support you. As we said in Question 2, you can't always control the people who are around you. However, you can make a conscious effort to gather your tribe of supportive people who help each other through the tough times and encourage each person to live well.

Dr. Restak talks about emotional contagion. If there were a room full of people who all had the flu and you had a choice whether to enter the room or not, would you enter? Probably not. And yet many times we choose to go hang out with people whose energy pulls us down.

Yes, we all have family members or work colleagues who may be described as "downers" or "negative Nellies." We can be caught in a trap of complaining about how things are not working in our lives, of playing a game of "I can top you" when discussing things like how busy we are or how tired we are. If you have friends who gossip about others, what will keep them from gossiping about you? While it is always wonderful to have friends who will listen to us when things aren't going well, do you have people who will hold space for you and support you to rise above what you are currently experiencing? Do you do the same for them? Sometimes there are people we need to limit our exposure to and others with whom we should be spending more time.

Carol: Twenty years ago, several of my dearest friends moved away from Los Angeles and I looked around and realized I needed to develop a new circle of friends. I also noticed some of the people I was hanging out with were not supportive of my goals and dreams. They spent a lot of time telling me why what I wanted wasn't possible or wouldn't work. I set the intention to gather a tribe of supportive friends. It didn't happen overnight. It meant getting out more and spending time with new people. Many of whom were nice people, just not "my people." But now looking around at my circle of "people," I am very happy to say I have a great tribe. We aren't perfect, we step on each other's toes at times but we are open and willing to laugh about being human.

Karen: I have had to find my tribe several times over the years. At one point, I noticed all my friends were through my work, and that my husband and I did not have any "couple friends." We made an effort to get to know people in our community through things like our son's T-Ball team, and settled into having a great social and support group. We went on family trips together, had barbeques in the summer, and our kids played hockey together. It was a wonderful time in our lives. But when our family experienced a particularly difficult period with one of our kids, this group fell quickly away. We weren't in the hockey tribe any longer, and I guess our best friends in the group were not equipped to support us in our new journey. It was easier for them to stay completely in that tribe. But now, many years on, I feel like Carol does about our tribe. We now know great people in several intersecting circles, and they are the right kind of tribe for us.

This is an area where the law of attraction works well. You have to be the person you want to attract. If you want more positive supportive interaction in life, you have to consciously create that within yourself. Asking the universe to help you find your tribe doesn't hurt either.

CHECK IN

Think about the conversations you routinely have at work or with your friends and family. Consider the quality of your conversation.

- How often do you sit and complain or gossip?

- How often do you participate in the "I Can Top You" game?

- Who are your supportive, positive peeps?

- How can you develop your support team?

- Is it time for a new tribe?

TAKE ACTION

- See if you can shift a conversation you regularly have with friends from the "busyness competition" or from complaining to talking about something that inspires you.

- Spend more time with the people who inspire you. Make a pact with your friends to provide mutual support for doing it!

- Send yourself a positive message on your phone or e-mail. Do this for your friends. Ask them to return the favor.

REPEATABLE

I choose supportive
and positive people
and grow my tribe.

QUESTION 18:
AM I MAKING ROOM FOR JOY AND PLAY?

"When we cultivate a relationship with our joy, our hearts and spirits expand and we remember who we are." Carol Woodliff

It is so easy to talk about managing all the parts of our lives and forget there is a very special sort of self-care — allowing yourself to have some time to enjoy life and doing something simply because you like it and it fills your heart.

Carol: I know many times when I am feeling out of sorts it is because I've become all about work. Even though I am self-employed and love my work, a life that is all about work doesn't feel supportive to me. I get grumpy and wonder, "What am I doing all this work for anyway?"

One of the things that absolutely fills me up is going to listen to live music. From a rock club on Sunset Strip, to folk music at a local guitar shop, to a symphony performance at the Hollywood Bowl, I am so fortunate to live in a city that provides me with these opportunities. Other people might think going to the

Viper Room to check out a new band would be torture. I love it and I find a piece of myself comes back home when I take myself out for this treat.

When I'm working with clients I often give them an assignment to go do something simply because it is fun! Many times they look at me with a blank expression on their face because they have lost their connection to the child who knew what fun was.

Karen: I have the same experience. Sometimes I even start to feel like the things I love to do are chores, and too hard to get done. But when I make time to take a hike with my husband out in nature, take pictures of the sunset, dig in the garden, or make art or jewelry, I lose sense of time and get quickly back to feeling whole and alive. Whenever I find it difficult to find time for these things, that is my signal to do one of them right away.

If we think back to when we were children, we had a natural sense of joy and play. Carol was walking by a park one day and there was a two-year-old little girl who was playing in the wood chips surrounding the swings. Her mom tried to put her in the swing and she protested with a loud squawk. The swing did not look as fun to her as picking up and throwing the wood chips. Fortunately she had a mom who shrugged her shoulders, sat down with her, and played with her on the ground. With that simple action, the mom taught her daughter that what she thought was fun was important.

How often do you forget to honor the essence inside you who knows what fun is?

CHECK IN

- Are you fun-deprived?

- Do you know what makes you happy?

- What is something silly you love to do?

- When was the last time you allowed yourself one of those moments?

TAKE ACTION

What is one thing you love to do you haven't given yourself permission to do in a while? Get out your calendar and plan it now. DO IT SOON.

Turn on some music you love and dance, sing (even if off key), play air guitar or conduct the symphony. Channel your childlike self who simply loves the song.

REPEATABLE

**Lighten Up!
Play is one of the
highest expressions
of my soul.**

QUESTION 19:
IS IT TIME FOR A BIG CHANGE?

"Every act of creation is first an act of destruction." Pablo Picasso

If you have been asking yourself all the questions up to this point in the book and are not experiencing a shift, it might be time to take a leap and make a BIG CHANGE. Maybe your job or relationships are causing you stress and no amount of "coping" will help. You are getting messages loud and clear it is time to move on. Perhaps the way you have been taking care of your health and fitness requires a BIG intervention. Maybe your spirit is asking you to change direction and embrace a more loving and courageous version of you.

When we connect with our hearts and spirits, we may know it is time, and yet we hesitate. Hesitation in itself can cause us stress. We often avoid those big changes because we don't feel ready. But every big change you have had to make in life feels this way. Making a major change like changing careers, moving cross-country or totally revamping your fitness and eating habits, doesn't happen all at once. But the change begins the moment you commit to that new goal.

We have noticed something interesting in our own lives and in the lives of clients: When it is time to make a change, the Universe keeps turning up the heat. Things start to nudge you to make the move. The boss asks you to take on a project that is more than you can complete in any reasonable timeframe and won't listen to your requests for help. You see friends making changes and moving in new directions and feel envy at their courage. Someone puts you on the spot with a tough question like, "Why are you still with him anyway?" You might notice and feel your resistance and reluctance to listen and take the needed steps. This can feel very stressful.

When we notice all those messages about how it is time to change and if we don't act, often the Universe acts for us with a nice big push!

Carol: Long after I had started my own business, I maintained ties with my former law firm working there part-time to supplement my income. I started to notice the difference in the energy between my healing practice and my law firm work. I needed to "shield up" to make it through a shift at the law firm job. There was a management turnover that meant the people who knew me the best and valued my contributions no longer worked for the firm. I started to notice my hours were being cut. It was no surprise when I soon got notice my contract was not being renewed. Why did all of this happen? I believe it happened because I wasn't paying attention to the messages that were saying, "This sort of work is no longer a fit for you." The Universe provided the "push out of the nest" for the leap that I wasn't making myself.

We notice the stress factor goes up for our clients when they are avoiding what is obvious. It is time for a new job, a big heart-to-heart talk with a spouse about the direction of a marriage, or many other big life issues.

There are certainly possible stressors in taking on the next big thing in life but ignoring the fact it is time to make a change will affect your energy and health in bigger ways than diving into the new challenges.

A good analogy here is learning to dive off the high dive. We don't know if you had the experience as a child of standing on the high dive looking down at the water with all the children behind you lined up. You weren't ready to dive in but you didn't have a choice, there were too many people on the ladder behind you, it was time to jump! The longer you waited the more stressful it became. This is what happens in life, the longer we avoid taking those steps toward the change calling to us, the more stressful it becomes. We may find ourselves tired and depressed because repressing the energy of change requires so much of our life force.

Karen: I was fed up with my corporate job and career, and had learned hypnotherapy, but was reluctant to even consider how I would ever leave the nest of a regular paycheck and subsidized benefits. It was scary! As I hung in there, several things occurred.

I had the opportunity to change departments within my company, and did it, thinking things would be better. I then got to work for a more difficult and insecure boss, who was doing his best to negotiate unfamiliar territory and change direction. The climate in the company grew tense and there were many closed-door meetings of top management. Interestingly, I then had several people from my workplace walk into my office and ask me to help them with hypnosis, and thus got some of my first paying clients. I still despaired of ever having a "way out." One day the sale of the company was announced, and along with it, the elimination of my department. It was so scary. But then I was offered a severance package, which allowed me to start my business and have some time to get it going. You never know what the universe has planned for you.

Big changes bring up all sorts of emotions. Many times, we call those emotions fear.

Carol: I studied and pursued acting for many years and I had a wise acting teacher tell me to be careful of how I labeled those emotions many call stage fright. She said you can label it stage fright and have it be a negative or you can label it excitement and use it as fuel for your performance. I have used this wisdom over and over again in my life when I am stepping into something new and it helps me recognize the butterflies uncertain feelings as a new curtain about to open in the "show" I call life.

You can change your experiences by changing your language.

Often times we are being called to a higher purpose and no amount of changing your thoughts about the current situation will do. This is the epic calling of the heroine's journey. Knowing you are doing the right thing for the right reasons can help you deal with stressful situations. We are all here to express ourselves as loving beings and that means we don't always get to take the easy route. Even though we have focused on personal stress in this book, there are times when we are called to step forward for our own development and the development of a better world.

Often we hide from our bigger missions due to fear. Our subconscious says "you can be great or safe" and we opt for safe. But our souls and spirit urge us to be more than the safe version of ourselves. When we ignore or hide from this, it can definitely cause pressure and uncomfortable feelings.

CHECK IN

- Have you had a sense you have a big mission and you have been avoiding it?

- What is your heart calling you to embrace?

- Where do you need courage to step forward?

- Are you ready to listen to your heart and soul's calling and ask for the courage to take the steps your heart asks you to take?

- Is there a big change calling to you that you have been ignoring?

- What are you telling yourself about the big change? Are you focusing on fear or excitement?

- What signs or signals do you notice that you may have been ignoring?

TAKE ACTION

What is one thing your heart and soul want you to say about that most loving and courageous you? Write an affirmation that helps you remember who you are and what your calling is such as:

- I listen to my heart and take the courageous steps in the direction of its calling.

- I love myself as I embrace this calling from my highest self.

Big change is an opportunity for you to vote for the type of life you want to live. In what ways is the big change asking you to think differently about your life?

Ask yourself, "What is the worst that can happen?" Very often, our fear makes us see all the dangers in opportunity. Are you really going to be destitute and living in a box if you take this leap? Or is the worst thing the fact you will have to get another corporate job for a while?

Ask yourself, "What is the BEST that could happen?" Create a vivid picture or description of how you want this new chapter of life to be.

- List 25 (or more) good things that can come out of this situation or change.

REPEATABLE

Whether fought or
embraced,
change is
a part of life.
I might as well take
the leap.

QUESTION 20:
AM I IN CRISIS?

"When written in Chinese the word 'crisis' is composed of two characters - one represents danger and the other represents opportunity." John F. Kennedy

When you are facing a major life challenge such as an illness, loss of a job, or divorce, you need to be realistic in your expectations and be kind to yourself. When the world has suddenly shifted under your feet, it can take some time to determine what the new normal is. Your ability to handle day-to-day tasks may be severely curtailed. Look at these major life challenges as time to sort your priorities. Do what you can and let the rest go for now.

Karen: I had been at my job only about six months when someone came into a meeting looking for me and said, "You need to call home right away." I went to my office and listened in a daze to at least five messages my husband had left as he handled the paramedics and ambulance ride for my two-and-a-

143

half-year-old son who had nearly drowned in our pool. I finally reached my husband and he told me to come directly to the emergency room. When something like this happens, you are immediately shocked into clearly knowing your priorities, and so is everyone around you. There was no issue with me leaving work, and I didn't give anything at the office or elsewhere a second thought as I drove the 20 miles to the hospital chanting aloud, "Breathe. Breathe. Breathe," to my son and to myself. When I got there, the chaplain was there. My son was unconscious and being slowly warmed up, while they monitored his vitals and lungs. They wanted to helicopter him to UCLA, but it was a foggy day, so we had to wait for an ambulance team to arrive and drive there, where he stayed in intensive care for a day. Ultimately, my son was fine, but many phases of the after-experience were hard for me. I felt guilty about receiving presents for him delivered to the house and meals cooked for us by church people I didn't know when he seemed so "fine" afterwards. I didn't want to leave him to go to work, and suddenly my job seemed so far from home. I worried constantly about something else happening and felt distracted at work. It took us all many months to regain our equilibrium, to believe our son was fine, and to feel comfortable taking him in the pool again. Normal didn't come back overnight.

As hypnotherapists and coaches, we saw clients all the time who said: "I'm going through a divorce, my mother is aging and I need to find other living arrangements for her, one of my children is acting out because of the divorce, I need to find a better job to support my family AND I want to quit smoking and lose 30 pounds in the next month." All we could say when these people came to us was "WHOA! You have a lot going on right now, let's slow down and handle one thing at a time." We don't mean to say you shouldn't exercise or focus on eating foods that are more healthful if that feels nurturing. Often when we get inspired to change our lives after a major event, we load ourselves up with too many big expectations. Only you know what is nourishing and what is too much!

Carol: Right after my father passed away, I was starting a new job and they asked if I wanted to delay my start date so I could have more time to grieve. I said no, I'll be fine—expecting I could handle all the major changes in my life—a death in the family, a move to a new city where I only knew two people, and a new job. I wasn't fine and then I beat myself up for making mistakes in my new job. The Universe also seemed to be piling on the stress. Someone smashed my car window to steal the stereo out of my car. I was assigned to work with a group of people who were known for being very demanding and hard to work with. My childhood pet passed away and then my 15-month-old niece passed away. I made many errors in my job during this time because I felt like the rug kept being pulled out from underneath me.

Some of the events like losing my father and niece are more traumatic than things like the car being broken into. However, sometimes it is the smaller things that break us. I remember sitting on the curb sobbing over my car. I never got "it" together to replace the stereo. When I traded the car in a year or so later, the huge hole in the dashboard was still there—a sign of my inability to cope with "one more thing" at that time of my life.

There are times in your life where you may feel like those inflatable BOZO™ punching bags many of us had as children. You begin to feel like you are coping and then something else happens, and "BAM!" it is as though you are punched again. You simply live moment-to-moment. You have no capacity to do more. You can appreciate how fragile life is and the beautiful moments you have had with those you have loved and lost. You can feel the conflicting mix of emotions. And you absolutely have to cut yourself some slack.

If you are in one of these situations, focus on handling the most pressing issues first. It may not be the best time to tackle the diet or quit smoking. It's okay to keep these on your future list, and concentrate on the most important thing for today.

Your ability to make decisions for your life is impacted when you have major emotional issues such as divorce or illness on your plate. When the world is shifting under your feet, it is important to be kind to yourself. Now is not the time to make hasty or unconsidered decisions or to use what is happening to you as a reason to beat yourself up. You are going through a tough time and you may not be at your best right now. Here are ways you can work with the ideas in this book in this challenging time.

- **First Things First.** Notice what you are juggling and what is important right now. Focus on the important stuff and gently put the rest aside for now (Question 10). Take the small steps you need to take, even if the step is something very simple like getting out of bed. Give yourself credit for taking those steps. (Question 16).

- **Call Out The Cavalry.** Ask for help in a big way! (Question 13) Let others support you. When they say, "Let me know what I can do," they mean it. Do you need them to make you dinner, do your laundry or . . .? Now take people up on their offers and if no one has offered, pick up the phone and ask. Someone may not step up to the plate but for each person who doesn't help out, you will be surprised about who will step forward. There are human angels all around us.

- **Call A Hotline.** Certain types of crisis situations need more immediate help than a self-help book can give you. If you are feeling depressed and suicidal or are experiencing domestic violence, here are a few toll-free hotlines in the United States that might be able to help. (If you are not in the United States, please reach out to the resources available in your country. You can find these resources by doing a web search for "suicide hotline" or "domestic violence hotline.") If you are dealing with one of those crisis situations, we hold you in love.

  - National Suicide Prevention Lifeline: 1-800-273-TALK (8255)
    http://www.suicidepreventionlifeline.org.

- The National Domestic Violence Hotline:
  1-800-799-7233
  http://www.thehotline.org

- **Turn To Your Faith/Spirituality.** Throughout this book, we've sprinkled tips about connecting with a higher power, the Universe, Spirit Guides or however you see those spiritual forces of love in the world. When it is all falling apart, we can surrender control to the higher power (Question 2) and pray or ask for help (Question 13). Prayer and meditation can be helpful when we feel like we have nowhere to turn or when we need support to keep us going.

- **Handle Your Basic Needs.** Perhaps you are familiar with Maslow's Hierarchy of Needs, which says when we are worried about safety or security we can't focus on higher goals like self-actualization. When you are in crisis, focus on your basic needs first. Make sure you are attending to food, shelter, sleep, etc. Perhaps all you can do today is focus on that, and also focus on breathing a little deeper to help the stress hormones flow out of your body.

- **Get a Second Set of Eyes and Ears.** When you are in crisis, it is hard to make good decisions. It can be hard to hear what advisors such as doctors or lawyers or are saying. Asking a friend to go with you to appointments such as a meeting with a doctor to discuss treatment options or to a funeral home to help plan a funeral, can help immensely. Having someone not quite so close to the situation hear what is being said and take notes for you often gives you more accurate information you can use later. This person can help remember questions you need to ask, and pay attention to things you may not be equipped to hear at the time.

- **Find a Sounding Board.** When you are overwhelmed with emotions, your sounding-board person can help you find a safe way to release all the energy created by those emotions. Having someone who can listen to you where you are can release stress right then and there. It can also help you gain another perspective which can give you access to new options. Make sure you connect with your tribe to help you keep a realistic perspective (Question 17).

- **Be Gentle in Your Expectations.** Know that your best today may not be what you normally would be able to do. Watch your assumptions (Question 3) and how you talk to yourself (Question 4).

- **Find Time to Feel.** Take a shower and cry. Punch a pillow, etc. Write a nasty letter to the situation! Yes, there may be times and places you need to be the strong one and hold it together, but it is equally important to allow yourself a time and place to grieve, be angry, frustrated and deal with the whole range of feelings you have. Honoring your feelings often helps relieve the grip they seem to have on you. Letting them have their say can be a great stress reliever (Question 14).

REPEATABLE

In times of crisis,
the nonessentials
fall away.
First things first.

CREATING YOUR PERSONAL PLAN

"Love yourself first, and everything else falls in line. You really have to love yourself to get anything done in this world."

Lucille Ball

Self-love is critical to bringing your best to the world. It is a form of self-love to continue to ask these questions and examine the answers regularly in your life. Discovering where you can ask a better question and shift your thoughts and energy is the most powerful gift you can give yourself. If you have worked through the questions in the book, you've discovered this yourself. If you read through the book, and thought, "This makes sense," we are asking you to go deeper and apply these questions to your life now.

You may not be an expert at the techniques yet, but each time you return to the questions, you will have those moments where you have a deeper personal insight into how your mind works. These insights are more important than what anyone else tells you. These 20 Questions may inspire you to create more questions that are important for you. Writing down your "aha" moments can help you remember them moving forward. What realizations did you have as you worked though this book?

WHAT I HAVE LEARNED USING THIS BOOK?

1.

2.

3.

4.

5.

6.

7.

8.

9.

10

.

YOUR PERSONAL PLAN

We invite you to implement a personal plan so you continue to train yourself to use your thoughts to enhance your experience and create your life in the best way for you. This is an invitation to play with the energy and keep the game going. It doesn't have to add burden to your life. It can free you to connect with your internal strength. We want to caution all you over-achievers out there: Only do what makes sense to you, don't over-do it, and know you can make a new plan at any time. If nothing else, remember this question above all others: **What is the best thing I can do for myself right now?**

Commit now to what you will do next.

What two questions do you feel you should focus on right now?

    1.

    2.

Re-read the corresponding chapters and identify the actions you will take:

    1.

    2.

    3.

    4.

List two simple things you can do to take care of you.

    1.

    2.

Open your calendar and schedule TIME FOR YOU. You need to carve out a time for these things, or even with the best of intentions, you won't do them.

You can return to the questions and action steps in this book again and again and revisit your plan whenever you like. As you develop your skills at asking questions to change your mind and taking care of yourself, you will become a more resilient you. We wish you love, peace, and wonder in your journey to reducing stress for good.

REPEATABLE

Do what works.
Let go of what
doesn't.

IF YOU LIKED THIS BOOK:

Please leave a review on Amazon, Goodreads, or your favorite online book review site.

Tell a friend. Buy her a copy of the book.

Share a post about it with your social media friends.

Blog about it. (We are available for blog tours or Podcast interviews!)

Start a group to work with these techniques with your friends.

Contact us to come speak to your women's event.

We welcome comments from readers. You can reach us at: Carol@CarolWoodliff.com or Karen@divineyoucrafts.com.

Check out Carol's book: *From Scared to Sacred: Lessons in Learning to Dance with Life* available on Amazon.com or other fine on-line retailers.

Karen invites you to consider a subscription to a Divine You Crafts monthly conscious crafting kit – part soul work, part craft, part fun – and let yourself play with the art of your life. Go to DivineYouCrafts.com to learn more.

ABOUT CAROL AND KAREN

A psychic once told us we were twins joined at the head in a past life and told us to meditate with our heads together. We tried it and couldn't stop laughing. We're not sure about the past life story but do cherish our connection wherever it came from.

We started out together with a professional development company called WMW Group, which provided wellness seminars to organizations and taught private seminars helping people quit smoking, manage stress and achieve their goals. While those seminars were fun, there was something missing. We let go of WMW Group so we could follow those deeper callings of our hearts. For a while, we went our separate ways in business, still remaining friends until a half-written stress book called us back and asked us to take another look at it. We realized we didn't want to focus on stress but how we can look beyond it; that's how *Stop Managing Stress!* was born.

Carol: I'm the author of the book, *From Scared to Sacred: Lessons in Learning to Dance with Life*. I believe life is a dance between our soul callings and our choices in life. There is so much available here for us to experience, I've never understood people who say, "There's nothing to do!" and I've always been a seeker of new experiences both in this world and spiritually. I am a shaman, healer, writer, and performer. I am a graduate of Marquette University, The Hypnosis Motivation Institute and the Healing The Light Body Program at The Four Winds Society. I have continued my studies with wisdomkeepers of many traditions. I love facilitating unique ceremonies to mark special occasions and set intentions. I share photos from my journey on my Facebook and Instagram pages: A Shaman on the Walk. I love to speak and perform and am currently writing a one-woman show. You can find me at:

> http:/CarolWoodliff.com or at
> http:/www.Facebook.com/CarolWoodliffauthor.

Karen: I am an artist and co-owner of Divine You Crafts, makers of monthly conscious crafting kits. We do magical events and parties, inspirational jewelry and more. With my husband Brian, I co-own Balance Point Spa in Santa Clarita, California where we provide treatments for body, mind and spirit. I am a graduate of San Francisco State University, the Hypnosis Motivation Institute, and also completed some graduate work at University of San Francisco. I love to help others be creative, connect to Spirit, and discover and contribute who they truly are. Contact Karen through:

> https://www.facebook.com/divineyoucrafts
> www.divineyoucrafts.com
> https://www.facebook.com/balancepointspa
> www.Balancepointspa.com

WITH MUCH GRATITUDE

To all the people we "picked" to be with us on this human journey this time around. We thank our family, friends, co-workers, bosses (good and challenging) and all those chance encounters who have taught us so much. This book would not be possible without you.

Thank you to our wonderful proofreaders, book group commenters and test drivers: Bridget Fonger, Pamela Koch, Annette Magee, Tina Ridener, Gail Palmer Ross, and Marie Stein. Thanks to Janell Mithani for always taking the best photos of us!

To you the reader, thank you for being part of our tribe and for buying this book.

www.ingramcontent.com/pod-product-compliance
Lightning Source LLC
LaVergne TN
LVHW092317080426
835509LV00034B/515